# CONRAD'S PREFACES

# CONRAD'S PREFACES
## TO HIS WORKS

*With an introductory essay by*
EDWARD GARNETT
*and a biographical note*
*on his father by*
DAVID GARNETT

BOOKS FOR LIBRARIES PRESS
FREEPORT, NEW YORK

First Published 1937
Reprinted 1971

INTERNATIONAL STANDARD BOOK NUMBER:
0-8369-5831-4


LIBRARY OF CONGRESS CATALOG CARD NUMBER:
72-160963


PRINTED IN THE UNITED STATES OF AMERICA

# EDWARD GARNETT: A BIOGRAPHICAL NOTE

My father, Edward Garnett, had finished writing the introduction to this book four or five days before he died. The fact of having finished it put him into a cheerful frame of mind at our last meeting, when he gave me a copy of it and asked me for my comments. Mr. Hugh Dent has suggested that I should write this biographical note. In my opinion Edward Garnett cannot be judged from anything he wrote. I do not mean that his plays, or his published criticisms (he reviewed the novels for many years in the 'Speaker' under the editorship of J. L. Hammond, and in the 'Nation' under that of H. W. Massingham), are in any way negligible. But from his writings no one would guess that he had been for over forty years a great influence in shaping other men's work. I shall try to explain, in a few words, how this came about.

Born in January 1868, Edward was the second son of Richard Garnett, keeper of printed books at the British Museum, and of Narney Singleton, his Irish wife. He was educated at the City of London School. The family background was an odd blend of Victorian respectability with complete liberality of opinion. The children were undisciplined and extremely untidy; only when they exhibited anything like worldliness or self-seeking were their parents surprised and shocked.

Edward grew into a lanky, idle, mischievous young man with a witty tongue and a quick temper. The spectacle of people who took themselves seriously—as at the Fabian Society, to which my mother introduced him—seemed to him irresistibly comic. He was a great swimmer and walked long distances, and had a certain cat-like agility which saved him broken bones. Faced with an angry bull, a dog with hydrophobia, or a homicidal lunatic, he behaved with a reckless physical courage, which was a measure of his exasperation.    I remember his picking up a live adder in his cap, and bringing it unharmed to a picnic to show us, when I was a child.

He got a job in a publisher's office when he was nineteen, and he married at twenty-one, soon after becoming Fisher Unwin's reader.    He remained a publisher's reader till his death, by which time he must have read as many manuscripts as any living man. His equipment for this task was not literary or academic, but a penetrating eye for character and a quick sympathy.    The early light-heartedness and unworldliness did not survive.    He found publishers posed as patrons of art and learning, though their absence of taste and illiteracy were the very reasons of his employ-ment, and their rapacity was blended with a ludicrous esteem of those authors who sold best.    Edward was a master of irony and his smile impaired complacency.    As a young man he must have been difficult for his employers, who made what should have been a shared adventure a matter for him of dangerous diplomacy. For, having discovered an author and got his first book published, Edward felt it his job to cajole and persuade him to write more and to develop his talent, though this might involve protecting the author from his own employer.

His relationship with Conrad was after this pattern, and Conrad has told the story of how Edward tempted him into writing his second book and thus prevented him from throwing up a literary career and going back to sea.

From the time of the Boer War to the Great War Edward found a sympathetic employer in Gerald Duckworth, who achieved merit by publishing Doughty's poetry as well as an abridgment of 'Arabia Deserta,' at what must have been a big loss.    But while he became more and more useful to certain writers, Edward suffered *from a feeling of isolation; this naturally led to irritability and exasperation. Since he never for a second doubted any of his critical judgments, he was also continually taking up the cudgels for those who were not appreciated. Often he denounced the absence of taste in the British public, in terms reminiscent of an evangelist rebuking the follies and vices of the fashionable world. This led to a bizarre turning of the tables when he was defending writers whose work had been accused of immorality. After the War, Edward's exasperation noticeably declined. Work, and particularly writing, which had been the very greatest effort to him, became far easier. He was lucky in his association with Jonathan Cape and on terms of warm friendship with all the partners of the firm. Moreover, the temper of the reading public had radically changed. Authors who had shocked the philistinism of the nineties, or who had seemed outlandish before the War, became best-sellers, justifying his early partisanship; after the War those he picked out often succeeded straight away.*

*In these later years a curious change of temperament showed itself in him. The impulsive, reckless, and frequently irritable Irish streak, which he inherited from his mother, seemed to disappear, while a shrewd and obstinate caution took its place. He spoke, too, with an authority which he had inherited directly from his father. In conversation he was extremely subtle, but this, the most characteristic quality of his mind, was called out only in his personal contacts and rarely appeared when he put pen to paper. He was unusually tolerant of vanity and egotism and treated young authors as the ideal producer has to treat theatrical stars. But when he felt they had gone wrong in their work, he would fight and flatter them until he often got his way. He was extremely sympathetic and easy to talk to about all personal matters. For, though he had all sorts of theories and prejudices, they ceased to exist when he was in contact with any one who* interested him. His interest in other people's characters was inexhaustible, completely unselfish, and very flattering. At the same time he could be extraordinarily crushing without realizing it, and his contempt was formidable. I must add that his deficiencies were quite unusual; he lacked the most ordinary bits of knowledge, but he knew instinctively the answers to problems which for many are insoluble.

*1937.*                                                    DAVID GARNETT.

# CONTENTS

# INTRODUCTORY ESSAY
## by Edward Garnett

# CONRAD'S PLACE IN ENGLISH LITERATURE

WRITING to Miss Collet from Saint-Jean-de-Luz, on 24th December 1902, George Gissing said:

> Read Conrad's new book. He is the strongest writer—in every sense of the word—at present publishing in English. Marvellous writing. The other men are mere scribblers in comparison. That a foreigner should write like this, is one of the miracles of literature.

The 'new book' was *Youth*, which contained two other stories also, *The Heart of Darkness* and *The End of the Tether*. This testimony from the most thorough-going of English realists, opens a door for the critic. The standard of literary quality in fiction in the nineties was poor. The crest of literary achievement in style and atmosphere had been reached by Stevenson's brilliant, versatile genius in historical romance, and beneath him were ranged a varied crew of middling late Victorian novelists, from Walter Besant to Mrs. Humphry Ward and Lucas Malet, from Clark Russell to Marion Crawford, from Barrie to Crockett, with dozens of other novelists, all strictly insular products, undefiled by foreign influences. Except in George Moore's *A Mummer's Wife*, French naturalism had gained no access to Albion's guarded shores. A Continental influence, in style and grace, had long been reflected in Henry James's subtle, accomplished pictures of the mental life of American and English characters moving in good society in London and Paris, and a superficial cosmopolitanism had indeed informed another American,

Marion Crawford (*Mr. Isaacs, Saracinesca*). The great
Russian novelists were only beginning to be available in
other than random, bad translations from the French.
Kipling's irruption in 1887, with *Plain Tales from the Hills*
and *Soldiers Three*, had broadened the horizon of the British
reader; the journalistic glorification of the British race,
hidden or loud in Kipling's books, was grateful to British
insularity. But the publication by Conrad of *Almayer's
Folly* (1895), *An Outcast of the Islands* (1896), *The Nigger
of the 'Narcissus'* (1897), *Tales of Unrest* (1898), *Lord Jim*
(1900), *Youth* (1902), not only threw a bridge between
the British public and the British sailors abroad and at home
and the Eurasian and native flotsam and jetsam in eastern
seas, *but a bridge between the British and the Continental spirit.*

In his Preface to *The Mirror of the Sea* Conrad says:
'Twenty years I had lived like a hermit with my passion'
(for the sea). And these twenty years at sea (1874–94)
had twisted a double strand in Conrad's work that has made
his achievement unique, one of special value to English
literature. These two chief strands are of course the
Continental and the English. For the English character
and spirit had been assimilated by the Polish writer, had
animated him and was portrayed by him as he had known
it on sea and land. Yet one must qualify this by stating
that the English element, preponderating in the sea novels,
almost disappears from our sight in others. Such an interweaving of spiritual qualities in fiction by a foreigner in the
English language handled by a master of style is un-
paralleled in English literature.

In *A Personal Record* (1912) Conrad has painted an
intimate picture of his Polish origins and of his ancestral
inheritance, as well as of his education and development

from his birth at Boerdiczew in Podolia on 3rd December 1857 to the day in 1878, in the port of Marseilles, when his hand touched for the first time the side of an English ship. With felicitous strokes Conrad indicates in the first twenty pages the stages by which he became an author and *Almayer's Folly* came into being. A square in Pimlico—the Congo—Geneva—the *Torrens*—Rouen— marked the growth and the vicissitudes of the manuscript, and while indicating these, Conrad sketches lightly the outline of his first seventeen years and of the twenty years of his seaman's wandering life which followed. In the second Preface to *A Personal Record* Conrad, after vindicating the memory of his father, Apollo Korzeniowski, a Polish patriot and a remarkable translator of Shakespeare, Victor Hugo, and Alfred de Vigny, defines 'the whole Polish mentality as one which had received its training from Italy and France and . . . in sympathy with the most liberal currents of European thought.' Thus he has himself declared for us that the basic constituents of his genius by blood and breeding were Polish, Latin, and French, while in the last lines of his book, in a glowing tribute to the English spirit and English seamen, he has exposed the English element he had adopted. 'I saw it suddenly flicker and stream out on the flagstaff. The Red Ensign . . . the symbolic, protecting warm bit of bunting flung wide upon the seas, and destined for so many years to be the only roof over my head.'

The Continental spirit in the works declares itself in the author's mentality, in which Slav psychological depth and Polish sardonic irony and fine susceptibility to every shade of feeling are mingled. A typical example of Conrad's ironical manner, which he inherited from his father, are

the pages devoted to his great-uncle Mr. Nicolas B., a
Napoleonic warrior, the recipient of the Polish Cross for
valour, who, on the retreat from Moscow, had devoured in a
dismal forest 'a luckless Lithuanian dog . . . in company
with two other military and famished scarecrows.'   Here
his sardonic reflections on the unpleasant fact are a scathing
comment on the immorality of a conqueror's ambition and
'the fate of that credulous (Polish) nation to starve for
upwards of a hundred years on a diet of false hopes and—
well—dog.'   His ironic cross-hatching of his subject, his
characters, and himself is foreign to the ordinary Anglo-
Saxon and appeared to others 'the most enigmatic side of
the author's nature,' though, temperamentally, it is, indeed, congenial to the Celt as we see in *The Songs of
Connacht* and Synge's plays.   But it is Slav in its uncompromising acceptance of the disconcerting fact.   'Il y a
toujours la manière,' quotes Conrad, and his sardonic
humour that enters into descriptions of people and events,
into his philosophic reflections, and into his personal attitude to life, is peculiarly individual.   It is the subtle twist
that presents a cutting edge in his comment, as we see in his
valedictory apology to the shade of Almayer in *A Personal
Record*, where he explains that if he, Conrad, had not
accepted 'a mumbled invitation to dine at his house' and
so 'got to know Almayer pretty well, it is almost certain
there would never have been a line of mine in print.   I
accepted then—and I am paying yet the price of my sanity.'
Almayer, 'the possesser of the only flock of geese on the
East Coast, is responsible for the existence of some fourteen
volumes so far.'   The most brilliant example of this gay
undercutting of his subject and his characters is 'The Duel'
which is the most Continental in colour, atmosphere, and

ironic spirit of all Conrad's long short-stories, and indeed for brilliancy and picturesque verve would be difficult to match in any language.   For that very reason, because it is Continental in its style of wit, it had the most insular reception with us, and was least acclaimed by the reviewers of any of Conrad's masterpieces.   W. L. Courtney, that donnish British critic who ruled the literary roost in the *Daily Telegraph* for many years, 'called *The Duel* tedious'! so Conrad wrote me on 21st August 1908, adding:

My first intention was to call that story *The Masters of Europe* but I rejected it as pretentious.   Anyway I did conscientiously try to put in as much of Napoleonic feeling as the subject could hold.   This has been missed by all the reviewers, every single one being made blind by the mere tale.

'The Duel' is a perfect example of Conrad's method of presenting complementary sides of the subject together, of showing the worn lining beneath the fabric of the coat. The fortunes of the young officers Lieutenant Feraud and Lieutenant D'Hubert in their frenzied encounters and vicissitudes and promotions on the battlefields of Europe typify the rise and glory and setting of the Napoleonic sun.   In their lives one sees its historic epitaph.   But the polished brilliance of the picture, its ironic wit, its sceptical gaiety were too Continental for the Briton who demanded 'plainer fare.'

But it is time to glance at Conrad's first books: *Almayer's Folly* (1895), *An Outcast of the Islands* (1896), *Tales of Unrest* (1898), consisting of five tales written in 1896–7. In his preface to *Almayer's Folly* Conrad defended 'that literature which preys on strange people' against the charge of being 'decivilized' brought against it by Mrs. Meynell, saying:

B

'I am content to sympathize with common mortals, no matter where they live; in houses or in tents, in the streets under a fog, or in the forests behind the dark line of dismal mangroves that fringe the vast solitude of the sea.'

And in the preface to *An Outcast of the Islands* he protests that though

it brought me the qualification of 'exotic writer' I don't think the charge was at all justified.   For the life of me I don't see that there is the slightest exotic spirit in the conception or style of that novel.   It is certainly the most *tropical* of my Eastern tales. The mere scenery got a great hold on me as I went on. . . .

Many readers at this date who had assimilated Kipling's *Soldiers Three*, *Wee Willie Winkie*, and Mrs. Hauksbee and the characters in *Plain Tales from the Hills*, undoubtedly thought the characters in *Almayer's Folly* and *An Outcast of the Islands* queer folk, outside the pale.   But the romantic setting of this outlandish native life, the adventures and picturesque atmosphere, appealed to the less insular 'honourable minority.'   Undoubtedly Kipling's example had paved the way for the 'exotic' Conrad's arrival, and the journalists were beginning to talk loosely about 'the fringes of the Empire.'   (Ten years earlier *The Purple Land that England lost* (1885) had received only one good review, so Hudson told me.)   And the publication of *An Outcast of the Islands* brought a handsome appreciation of 'the new writer' from Mr. H. G. Wells.   The tide was turning quietly in Conrad's direction, but how slow was its flow!   Four of the five stories in *Tales of Unrest* (1898) had been serialized in magazines, and in January 1899 the book gained a fifty-guinea prize from the *Academy* (chiefly Mr. E. V. Lucas's doing).   All these first books of Conrad were patently imbued with the foreign spirit, and while 'The Idiots' (a tale of the Brittany coast) was obviously in the manner of Maupassant, 'An Outpost of Progress,' a tale of the Congo, directly challenged the fashionable imperialistic propaganda and Kipling's gospel of 'the White Man's burden.'

But in the next three years (1898, 1899, 1900) Conrad entered a new phase of his literary development. In September 1896 he had returned with his wife from their stay in Brittany with the first part of *The Rescue* (the novel which he abandoned in despair and laid aside till 1918), and ten pages of *The Nigger of the 'Narcissus.'* After three months of harassing cares, *The Nigger* was finished on 10th January 1897,[1] and in this book and the three following, *Lord Jim*, *Youth*, and *Typhoon*, the English element in the literary fabric became conspicuous as, *Heart of Darkness* excepted, they were largely concerned with English seamen and English ships. *The Nigger of the 'Narcissus'* was a new departure in sea literature. Marryat, indeed, had drawn realistically the life of naval officers and men in frigates, on the home seas, in foreign ports, or in tropical waters, but his narrative was an externalized breezy and vivacious chronicle. But Conrad in *The Nigger* fuses the human life on board the sailing ship with sea and wind and weather into an integral whole. The gale off the Cape and the ship's peril from foundering is great prose and truly epical. Never before had the sea's fury and a crew's extremity and fortitude been described with such actuality, or with such beauty of style. The literary method was really that of the great Russian masters, Turgenev and Tolstoy. It was the Slav psychological method, now applied to the ship life of English seamen; but Conrad added something of his own in his treatment— 'his special poetic sense for the psychology of scene in

[1] *Letters from Joseph Conrad, 1895–1924*, p. 67. The Nonesuch Press (1928).

which the human drama before us is seen in just relation
to the surrounding forces of Nature.' The ostensible
subject, the malingering negro, James Wait, his illness
and death and the crew's incipient mutiny, is merely the
central peg on which this bundle of life is hung. But
the storm itself, the terror and fury of the great wave, the
ship's desperate straits, and the master, Captain Allistoun's
hoarse, sudden command: ' Wear ship . . . get the men
along! What's the matter with them?' incarnating the
tough spirit of the British sailor, these things Conrad
celebrated as no writer had done before him. The mate,
Mr. Baker, Singleton the old sailor, Archie the boy, the
cook, the boatswain, and Donkin the shirker, all these are
realistically treated, but all are, also, 'ideal figures' in this
'romance of reality.' Donkin, the snarling, gutter-bred
Cockney, is the Thersites of the piece. The devotion of
the crew to the sick nigger has been questioned, but even
if this be a flaw, *The Nigger* none the less holds its place as
a great sea classic.

In his apostrophe to England, as the *Narcissus* is racing
up the Channel, Conrad has defined the spiritual tie that
bound him for twenty years to the merchant service, a
tie that crystallized, later, in his fame and place in English
literature:

A great ship! For ages had the ocean battered in vain her
enduring sides; she was there when the world was vaster and
darker, when the sea was great and mysterious, and ready to
surrender the prize of fame to audacious men. A ship mother
of fleets and nations! The great flagship of the race; stronger
than the storms! and anchored in the open sea.

This is a passage of great rhetoric and true poetry written
from the heart. And the closing description of the paying-

off of the crew of the *Narcissus* and their dispersing on Tower Hill is one of the most moving tributes to British sailors ever written.

But at the corner I stopped to take my last look at the crew of the *Narcissus*. They were swaying irresolute and noisy on the broad flagstones before the Mint. They were bound for the Black Horse, where men, in fur caps with brutal faces and in shirt-sleeves, dispense out of varnished barrels the illusions of strength, mirth, happiness; the illusion of splendour and poetry of life, to the paid-off crews of southern-going ships. From afar I saw them discoursing, with jovial eyes and clumsy gestures, while the sea of life thundered into their ears ceaseless and unheeded. . . .

. . . A gone shipmate, like any other man, is gone for ever; and I never met one of them again. But at times the spring-flood of memory sets with force up the dark River of the Nine Bends. Then on the waters of the forlorn stream drifts a ship—a shadowy ship manned by a crew of Shades. They pass and make a sign, in a shadowy hail. Haven't we, together and upon the immortal sea, wrung out a meaning from our sinful lives? Good-bye, brothers! You were a good crowd. As good a crowd as ever fisted with wild cries the beating canvas of a heavy foresail; or tossing aloft, invisible in the night, gave back yell for yell to a westerly gale.

This, the closing passage in *The Nigger*, is quoted to show Conrad's literary method and to define his aims in 'the romance of reality.' In the foreground is the realist: 'They were bound for the Black Horse, where men, in fur caps with brutal faces and in shirt sleeves, dispense out of varnished barrels the illusions,' etc. In the background is the poet and the dreamer. 'Haven't we, together and upon the immortal sea, wrung out a meaning from our sinful lives? Good-bye, brothers!' And the last lines fuse with their sensuous imagery man and the

elements. 'You were a good crowd. As good a crowd
as ever fisted with wild cries the beating canvas of a heavy
foresail, or tossing aloft, invisible in the night, gave back
yell for yell to a westerly gale.'

It is, of course, the method of the poets, one especially
favoured by Shakespeare, this interweaving of images of
reality, philosophic reflections, and musing asides, with
sensuous impressions. But no Englishman has ever in
describing sea life conjoined such sensitive perception
with such breadth of vision as Conrad showed both in *The
Nigger*, in his next volume *Youth*, and, later, in *Typhoon* and
*The Mirror of the Sea*. The first story in *Youth* was induced
by a feeling so 'genuine' and so 'strong' that 'it poked
itself through the narrative, which it certainly defaces in a
good many places,' wrote Conrad apologetically to H. G.
Wells, 6th September 1898. And this is interesting to
note since in the second story, *Heart of Darkness*, we find
that 'the feeling,' no less genuine and strong, affects us
more subtly while the story artistically attains more searching effects. *Youth*, a marvellous paean to youth and 'the
days when we were young at sea; young and had nothing, on
the sea that gives nothing, except hard knocks,' mounts in an
emotional crescendo from the first to the last page. The
obscure heroes of the narrative are old Captain Beard and
Mahon, the aged, white-bearded mate, and the unnamed seamen who man 'the tired old ship,' the *Judea*, on the voyage
to Bangkok, which it never reaches, since after repeated
breakdowns in home waters the *Judea* takes fire in the
Indian Ocean and the crew, 'a lot of profane scallywags
who stuck it out,' save themselves in the boats and reach
a small Eastern port at night. The young mate's waking
vision of the men of the East is one of the most famous of

Conrad's descriptions. I quote a dozen lines here to recall
Conrad's magic to the memory:

> I was lying in a flood of light, and the sky had never looked
> so far, so high, before. I opened my eyes and lay without
> moving.
> And then I saw the men of the East—they were looking at me.
> The whole length of the jetty was full of people. I saw brown,
> bronze, yellow faces, the black eyes, the glitter, the colour of an
> Eastern crowd. And all these beings stared without a murmur,
> without a sigh, without a movement. They stared down at the
> boats, at the sleeping men who at night had come to them from
> the sea. Nothing moved. The fronds of palms stood still against
> the sky. . . . This was the East of the ancient navigators, so
> old, so mysterious, resplendent and sombre, living and un-
> unchanged, full of danger and promise. And these were the men.

Here the evocation of things seen in memory hangs upon
the cadence of its utterance, one both musical and rhetorical
in the rise and fall of the speaker's emotion. Here, too,
the emotion rises in a crescendo, till, subdued in the closing
lines, it passes into a dying fall.

*Heart of Darkness*, the second tale in *Youth*, was of European importance. In it Conrad, drawing on his own
experiences in the Congo, had put in a long short-story
what scores of travellers and investigators affirmed about the
enslavement of the Congo peoples by their Belgian masters.
But what reports and the evidence of Blue Books cannot
do, *Heart of Darkness* did, by catching the infinite shades of
deterioration in the white man's morale when he is freed
from European restraint and planted down in the tropics
to make trade profits out of black subject races. The
masterly picture of the fantastic relations of civilization
with the primitive barbarism of Africa is conveyed in a
sustained narrative of the most sombre hues. As always

with Conrad, the spiritual is conveyed through the thing done, seen, and suffered. We see the stillness of the brooding African forests, the glare of the sunshine, the feeling of dawn, of noon, of night on the tropical river, and we feel the mental isolation of the degenerating unnerved whites every day facing the Heart of Darkness which threatens their own creed and conceptions, the fatalism of the bewildered savages in the grasp of the rapacious officials, the white 'workers for progress.' The note of ill omen is first struck by Marlow's impressions when he is signing his contract at the great trading company's offices in Brussels, 'a whited sepulchre,' and is scrutinized by two women door-keepers knitting black wool and scanning the applicants' faces with unconcerned old eyes. And the warning note deepens during Marlow's voyage down the ominous African coast with its suggestion of 'some sordid farce acted in front of a sinister back-cloth.' Such is the sight of the French man-of-war at anchor, idly shelling the empty bush. 'It appears the French had one of their wars going on thereabouts.' Sometimes the note is of ironic grimness, as when Marlow comes across the remains of his predecessor, Fresleven, who had been stabbed by a native over a quarrel about two black hens!

. . . the grass growing through his ribs was tall enough to hide his bones. They were all there. The supernatural being had not been touched after he fell. And the village was deserted, the huts gaped black, rotting. . . . The people had vanished. Mad terror had scattered them, men, women, and children, through the bush, and they had never returned. What became of the hens I don't know either. I should think the cause of progress got them, anyhow.

The astonishing delicacy and force of Conrad's artistic

touch is seen in Marlow's description of the grove of death, 'the gloomy circle of some inferno,' where the worn-out natives have crawled to die, while the work of building a railway is going on:

They were dying slowly—it was very clear. They were not enemies, they were not criminals, they were nothing earthly now—nothing but black shadows of disease and starvation, lying confusedly in the greenish gloom. Brought from all the recesses of the coast in all the legality of time contracts, lost in uncongenial surroundings, fed on unfamiliar food, they sickened, became inefficient, and were then allowed to crawl away and rest. These moribund shapes were free as air—and nearly as thin. I began to distinguish the gleam of eyes under the trees. Then, glancing down, I saw a face near my hand. The black bones reclined at full length with one shoulder against the tree, and slowly the eyelids rose and the sunken eyes looked up at me, enormous and vacant, a kind of blind, white flicker in the depths of the orbs, which died out slowly.

And so the picture of tragic imbecility and human rapacity is built up scene after scene to its poetical climax. 'That sombre theme had to be given a sinister resonance, a tonality of its own, a continued vibration that, I hoped, would hang in the air and dwell on the ear after the last note had been struck,' Conrad says in his preface to *Youth*, and one's only question is as to whether the central figure, the sadistic Kurtz, the apex and culmination of the white man's moral deterioration, is not over-emphasized as a symbol of 'the horror.' 'The horror! The horror!' is Kurtz's final cry after his face has expressed pride, power, terror, and his triumph in gratifying his passions with the bodies and souls of the natives he has tortured. Marlow's final scene in Brussels with Kurtz's 'intended lady' has the note of brooding irony peculiar to Conrad, and the closing scene on the Thames has the effect of poetry that 'seemed to lead into the heart of an immense darkness.'

While *Heart of Darkness*, in its ironic exposure of the white man's civilized inhumanity and its sombre vision of Nature's elemental darkness, was antithetic to the comfortable insularity of contemporary English fiction, in Conrad's description of the world map hanging in the office of the great Congo Company are two lines attesting the link he had forged with the enterprising British spirit overseas: 'There was a vast amount of red—good to see at any time, because one knows that some real work is done in there.' And in his next book, *Lord Jim*, Conrad wove out of the foreign warp and English weft the famous novel that has perhaps appealed most to English sentiment, because it presented or seemed to present a moral issue.   Its hero, Jim, the young English officer, was 'one of us,' 'a gentleman,' who had dishonoured the English name by deserting his sinking ship, jumping in panic into the boat which left the helpless Arab pilgrim passengers to their fate.   'The tragic and disgraceful story of the abandoned pilgrim ship, the *Patna*, was a memory in that quarter of the Eastern sea that caused us to blush for our race,' says Sir Hugh Clifford.   In treating this subject Conrad chose one that demanded the finest analysis of a man's impulses and behaviour in a crisis, and a dissection of hidden flaws in character that may destroy his morale. Our English attitude to the dishonoured Jim is well illustrated by the behaviour of Captain Brierly, the captain of the crack ship of the Blue Star Line, and one of Jim's judges at the official inquiry, who at first asks: ' Why are we tormenting that young chap?' but afterwards says to Marlow: 'Let him creep twenty feet underground and stay there.'   A side-

light is thrown on the perplexities that attend the delivery
of judgment on our fellows when Captain Brierly, who was
'second to none' and 'who presented a surface as hard as
granite,' deliberately jumps overboard at sea, a week after
the inquiry. Why? 'The heart of another is a dark
forest,' says the proverb, and Captain Brierly's question is
the danger-signal before his suicide. One of the finest
examples of Conrad's literary craftsmanship is the scene
and the talk between Marlow and the old French naval
lieutenant on the matter of 'honour' and the future of a
man who, having succumbed to fear and let everything go,
'has got to live with that fear of himself—when the honour
is gone.' The course of Jim's redemption is foreshadowed
in his reply to Marlow: 'I may have jumped, but I don't
run away.' Conrad's success in the working out of Jim's
problem has been variously estimated by his critics. One
may quote the opinion of Sir Hugh Clifford, himself an
authority on Malayan life: 'I know of no work of Conrad's
that conveys with more mysterious success so poignant an
impression of the Malayan Archipelago. *Lord Jim*, his most
sustained effort, approaches as near to perfection, I think,
as it is given to mere mortal to attain.' Side by side with
this eulogy may be set Conrad's disclaimer in a letter to
me, 20th January 1900, in answer to my praise of the early
part of the narrative: 'the truth is that it is not my depth
but my shallowness that makes me so inscrutable. Thus
(I go cold to think) the surprise reserved for you will be
in the nature of a chair withdrawn from under one.' [1]
Later he wrote that he had been 'satanically ambitious
. . . what is fundamentally wrong with the book [is] the
want of illuminating imagination. I wanted to obtain a
sort of lurid light out of the very events.' [2] To what

[1] *Letters from Conrad*, pp. 164.     [2] Ibid., p. 172.

degree Conrad did obtain this 'lurid light' out of the last
acts of the quixotic Jim, and his determination and death,
will be answered according to the reader's temperament.
It may be assumed that Sir Hugh Clifford's verdict is the
typical English one.   The consummate mirage of Malayan
life, with its rich and intricate drama of Patusan intrigue,
blends with and throws a slight haze over Jim's romantic
character.   Critics may be left to ponder the difficult
question of the nature of 'illuminating imagination.'   But
the writer's view is that in *Lord Jim*, Jim's actions and words
and thoughts are not so convincing in themselves as the
poetic conception of his figure placed by fate and his one
great *défaillance*, in his role of the wanderer of the Eastern
seas.   It is the whole mirage in which we are enveloped
that makes *Lord Jim* so triumphant a piece of art.

In his preface to *Typhoon*, the story which followed
*Lord Jim*, Conrad is more explicit than usual about his aim
and literary method.   He says that:

Years before I had heard it being talked about in the East as
a recent occurrence. . . . Yet it was but a bit of a sea yarn
after all.   I felt that to bring out its deeper significance which
was quite apparent to me, something other, something more was
required: a leading motive that would harmonize all these violent
noises, and a point of view that would put all that elemental
fury into its proper place.

What was needed of course was Captain MacWhirr.   Directly
I perceived him I could see that he was the man for the situation.
I don't mean to say that I ever saw Captain MacWhirr in the
flesh, or had ever come in contact with his literal mind and dauntless temperament.   MacWhirr is not an acquaintance of a few
hours, or a few weeks, or a few months.   He is the product of
twenty years of life. My own life.   Conscious invention had
little to do with him.

The   unshakable   MacWhirr   in   his   unimaginativeness

and iron-nerved matter-of-factness is indeed a Briton to be proud of, and his scenes with the impressionable critical mate, Mr. Jukes, and the Chinese coolies are ironic comedy of a most original kind. As to the unerring realism with which the approach and bursting of the typhoon, its impact on the ship, and its physical effects on the crew are treated, one can only say that no description so vivid and so veracious in detail can be found to match it. One may note that in his sketches of the wives of the captain and the first engineer, Mrs. MacWhirr and Mrs. Rout, Conrad has shown most intimate observation of the women at home and the domestic atmosphere awaiting the British seaman on his return from a voyage.

In *Amy Foster*, the story that followed *Typhoon*, Conrad passed from British seamen to English village life. Gissing wrote to him, on 9th May 1903:

*Amy Foster* (I remember your mentioning the subject when I was with you) takes great hold upon me—as pathetic a thing as can be found in literature. Admirable the contrast between the creature of a far-off land, a man of dreams and passion, and subtle joys, and the stodgy villagers of matter-of-fact England. Amy is a wonderful study in elementary womanhood—oh! how I see her! and your atmosphere—the chill, briny odour—Ah! ever present sounding of the sea!

Any one who has lived in a Kentish or Sussex village thirty years ago will recognize the deep-seated hostility of the slow-moving rural folk to the outlandish looks and ways and manners of strangers who come amongst them and will know how true to life is the story of Yanko, the ship-wrecked foreigner from the Carpathians. The atmosphere of village tap-rooms and Baptist chapels, of farm buildings and middens, of cottages and sheepfolds, both blankets and isolates the wondering Yanko, who in the end, when lying sick and helpless, excites the repulsion and the ungovernable fear of his girl wife, Amy, so that she leaves him, the 'strange man,' to die alone in his delirium. Again it is both in the strange union of foreign and insular feeling, of universal appeal and atmospheric illusion of Brenzett's stolid life that *Amy Foster* turned fresh furrows in English fiction of the period.

In *A Personal Record* Conrad gives a faithful account of how for twenty months he had 'wrestled with the Lord' for his next creation, *Nostromo*, 'for the headlands of the coast, for the darkness of the Placid Gulf, the light on the snows, the clouds on the sky and for the breath of life that had to be blown into the shapes of men and women, of Latin and Saxon, of Jew and Gentile.' In this tale of 'an imaginary but true seaboard,' Conrad, as Mr. Mégroz tells us, 'had practically no facts at all to go on. He landed twice for a few hours in 1875 and 1876 on his two trips in the *Saint-Antoine* at ports in the Gulf of Mexico. . . . As Conrad wrote despondently to a friend, he had drawn upon every scrap of his knowledge of South American republics, using everything, rejecting nothing. And it does not seem to matter in the least. Nowhere else shall we find more convincing concreteness of objects or more vivid light and shade.' One critical generalization deducible from *Nostromo* is that fidelity to geography and topography is of secondary importance in Conrad's fiction; it happens to be fairly constant merely because of his autobiographical record. He never confused literal truth with imaginative truth.

Naturally not. But is there enough sharpness of topographical reality in the great mirage of *Nostromo*, a romance

which is the artistic quintessence of both Central American
and South American States?   If we are to judge Conrad by
the high-water mark of his art, is not *Nostromo* too genera-
lized a picture?[1]   Apart from this there is scarcely a line
in the book that is not essential to the development of this
dramatic pageant of life.   The theme is not indeed the life
and death of the hero, Nostromo, El Capataz de Cargadores,
neither is it the story of the vicissitudes of the great San
Tomé silver mine and of the Europeans who develop it in
Sulaco.   Conrad's artistic instinct led him to clear the
reefs of these subsidiary issues and bring him and his
readers safe into the open sea, whence they can look back
at the bold outline of the Costaguanan coast, the placid
waters of the Golfo Placido, and realize that his subject is
the great mirage he has conjured up of the life and nature
of the Costaguana territory lying under the shadow of
the mighty Cordilleras.   The foreground of Nostromo is,
indeed, the drama of the political and revolutionary vicissitudes of the town of Sulaco, of the struggle between the
rival Monterist and Ribierist factions, the latter allied with
the interests of the European and American capitalists who
have developed the silver mines, introduced the service of
the O. S. N. Shipping Co., and projected the National
Central Railway.   At the period when the tale opens the
Monterist faction is just gaining the upper hand and is
thirsting to cut the throat of every prominent Moderate or
Ribierist in Costaguana.   The story of the street-fighting
and the suppression of Gamacho and his Nationals by the
mixed group of Europeans and Ribierists with Nostromo,
the magnificent Capataz, who leads his body of Cargadores

[1] For the contrary view, see Edward Crankshaw's critical appreciation
and eulogistic dissection of the first chapter of *Nostromo* in *Joseph Conrad*,
pp. 181–9 (1936).

against the town rabble and then hastily takes out to sea a
lighter with its cargo of silver ingots just in time to escape
the raid of Colonel Sotillo and the revolted garrison of
Esmeralda, while Pedro Montero and his cut-throats sweep
into the town from the mountains—all this is told us
through the medium of various characters such as Captain
Mitchell, the pompous old resident officer of the O. S. N.
Co.; Nostromo himself; Martin Decoud, Spanish creole,
Parisian boulevardier, and Ribierist journalist; Doctor
Monygham, a broken and gloomy army doctor, who has
seen too much of Costaguana and its revolutions to have
any illusions left; and indirectly through the medium of
Mrs. Gould, the wife of the mine-owner; Giorgio Viola, an
old Garibaldian soldier; and Colonel Sotillo, military bravo,
and torturer of the miserable Hirsch, the German Jew.
Conrad never before or after attempted to group together
such a variety of characters, to exhibit so many conflicting
issues.   How was he able to do it, and what is the nature
of the artistic method by which scene after scene flows
clearly, freely, in natural and convincing sequence, leaving
the impression on the reader of having seen and assisted at
a national drama?

   In Conrad's vision we are shown Nature as a ceaselessly
flowing river of life, out of which the tiny atom of each
man's individual life emerges into sight, stands out in the
surrounding atmosphere, and is lost again in the infinite
succession of the fresh waves of life.   Thus Conrad's pre-
eminence lies specifically in the delicate relation of his
characters to the whole environment—to the whole mirage
of life in which their figures are seen to move.   The
character-drawings of Mrs. Gould and Dr. Monygham,
Captain Mitchell and old Viola, though admirable studies,

cannot be called particularly original creations; but their human significance is great if we consider them as figures which serve as arresting points by which we can focus the character of the national drama around them and penetrate to the larger drama of Nature. Thus, while the psychology of certain characters, as Charles Gould, Decoud, and Nostromo himself, is by no means always clear and convincing, when we take the figure of Mrs. Gould and analyse the effect made on us by the vision of her exquisite and gracious nature, moving 'with her candid eyes very wide open, her lips composed into a smile,' amid the electric and sullen atmosphere of this South American town, weighed down by the ever-hanging menace of her husband's danger, ministering to all in turn who seek her ear, while conscious in secret that her husband, in his fanatical devotion to the interests of the San Tomé mine, has surrendered, merged, and lost sight of his love for her—if we consider the spirit of this woman we shall recognize how exquisitely just is the author's sense of perspective which has led him to place her so that, like a figure in a landscape, she serves as the gleam of light against the sombre and threatening horizon. And in the same way the Spanish-American revolutionary rabble of Sulaco shows up 'sullen, thievish, vindictive, and bloodthirsty' against the devotion to duty of Giorgio Viola, the old Garibaldian hero. And thus against the woodenheaded unimaginativeness of the Britisher, Captail Mitchell, the hardheaded idealism of Charles Gould, and the gloomy disillusionment of Dr. Monygham, the whole racial genius of this captivating and gracious South American land, semi-barbarous, with its old-world, Spanish traditions and its 'note of passion and sorrow,' stands forth triumphantly;

c

and its atmosphere penetrates to our European consciousness.   And if this is so—if in Conrad's art the whole
mirage of Nature, the series of flowing scenes in which are
reflected the subtly shifting tides of human emotion and
human passion, are everything—we shall see why it is
that the artistic imperfections of some of his figures are
of curiously little importance.   It is because with most
writers the whole value of the scene is centred in their
characters, but with Conrad the value is in the whole
panorama, in which the figures are, strictly speaking, the
human accessories.

Our survey of Conrad's work so far shows that his genius
hangs upon his power of seizing the essential characteristics
and features of an environment and his power of portraying
the characters that people the human drama he had either
met in life or arrived at creating.   His sensitive impres-
sionability and receptivity to the forces of nature and the
character of the life surrounding is conjoined with an acute
realization of the spirit of men, of the species of man the
individual before him belongs to—whether the scene be in
Malaya, the Congo, South America, Marseilles, London, a
Kentish village, or on board ship.   The range of Conrad's
vision and the justness of his insight are revealed in his
novel *The Secret Agent* (1907), a story of the subterranean
life of a London environment.   In his preface to the
novel his account of how it came into being through the
chance remark of a friend and a passage in the book of
an assistant commissioner of police, and how in three days
'the story of Winnie Verloc stood out complete . . . ready
to be dealt with'—is a most illuminating instance of the
processes in his work of creation, with the result that the
fashioning of the novel reveals a combination of qualities,

psychological and philosophical, that are not within the compass of English writers.  London, Scotland Yard, Soho, and its denizens are indeed common ground.  Winnie Verloc and her brother Stevie, Chief-Inspector Heat and his chief, the assistant-commissioner, are English characters, but the two bureaucrats, M. M. Vladimir and Wurmt of the foreign embassy, Mr. Verloc the *agent provocateur* and the anarchists, Michaelis, Karl Yundt, Comrade Ossipon and the professor, are obviously figures that seem unworthy of our British sympathies—and that is precisely where Conrad's philosophy, impartial in its scrutiny of human nature, showed his superiority to his English contemporaries who held openly or secretly an ethical brief.  His superiority is shown in the impartiality which, facing imperturbably all the conflicting impulses of human nature, refuses to be biassed in favour of one species of man rather than another.  Chief-Inspector Heat, the thief-taker and the guardian of social order, is no better than the inflexible avenger of social injustice, the Professor.  The Assistant Commissioner of Police, though a fearless and fine individual moves our admiration no more than does the child-like idealist, Michaelis, who has been kept in prison for fifteen years for a disinterested act of courage.  Whether the spy, Mr. Verloc, is more contemptible than the suave and rosy-gilled favourite of London drawing-rooms, M. Vladimir, is as difficult a point to decide as whether the latter is less despicable than the robust seducer of women, the cowardly Comrade Ossipon.  And, by a refined stroke of irony, the innocent victim of anarchist propaganda and bureaucratic counter-mining is the unfortunate and weak-witted lad, Stevie, whose morbid dread of pain is exploited by the bewildered *agent provocateur* Mr. Verloc, in his efforts to

serve the designs of his embassy, and to keep his job and
to save his own skin.   Finally, as an illustration of our
author's serene impartiality, we may mention that the
real heroine of the story is concealed in the trivial figure
of Mr. Verloc's mother-in-law, whose effacement of self
for the sake of her son, Stevie, is the cause contributory
to his own and her daughter's ruin.   For Mr. Verloc,
growing desperate, sends the half-witted lad with an in-
fernal machine to blow up Greenwich Observatory, and,
Stevie perishing, Mr. Verloc is attacked by his wife in a
fit of frenzy and killed.

While the psychological analysis of the characters' motives
is as full of acumen as is the author's philosophical penetra-
tion into life, it is right to add that Mr. Verloc and his wife
are less convincing in their actions than in their meditations.
There is a hidden weakness in the springs of impulse of both
these figures, and at certain moments they become auto-
mata.[1]   But such defects are few.   Conrad's art of sug-
gesting the essence of an atmosphere and of a character in
two or three pages was never more strikingly illustrated
than in *The Secret Agent*, which has the profound and ruthless
sincerity of the great Slav writers mingled with a haunting
charm that recalls his compatriot Chopin.

A further example of Conrad's extreme receptivity is
manifest in the novel *Under Western Eyes* (1911).   I unjustly

---

[1] With reference to this critical opinion expressed in a review in 1907,
Conrad wrote me at the time: 'I am no end proud to see you 've spotted
my poor old woman.   You 've got a fiendishly penetrating eye for one's
most secret intentions. . . . And you are so appallingly quick in jumping
upon a fellow.   Yes.   Oh, yes! my dear Edward—that 's what 's the matter
with the estimable Verloc and his wife,' the hidden weakness in the springs
of impulse.   'I was so convinced that something was wrong there that to
read your definition has been an immense relief—great enough to be akin
to joy.'—*Letters from Conrad*, p. 211.

charged Conrad with putting hatred into the book and after re-reading the story twenty-five years later, I own I was wrong. In writing to my sister Olive, Conrad said: 'The fact is that I know extremely little of Russians. Practically nothing. . . . In the book, as you must have seen, I am exclusively concerned with ideas.' [1] This is too modest. In his picture of the Russian revolutionary circle in Geneva, Conrad has drawn types of revolutionaries that did exist and that maybe will come into being again, in another century and in another Geneva. Whence Conrad got his characters, Razumov, Councillor Mikulin, Haldin, Ziemi-anitch, Prince K., Peter Ivanovitch, Madame de S., Laspara, Nikita, Tekla, and Sophia is obvious. All that he had known and that his family had known and suffered at Russian hands, all that he had read and brooded deeply over, he put together with care and exactitude, and without artistic prejudice. The picture of the revolutionary circle incarnates his convictions on the nature of the Russian, his character and the workings of his mind. That there should be national prejudice in the picture and deep-lying distaste was inevitable, but it is remarkable that the characterization of these Russian types should be as penetrating as it is. Looking back on the period, 1907, when it was written, in the light of all that has happened since, one sees how admirable is the atmosphere and perspective of the picture, though Miss Haldin is the weakness of the book. As Conrad admitted, 'that girl does not move.' As to Razumov himself, about this truly Russian hero there is something to me inconclusive. But, on the other hand, Peter Ivanovitch, 'the revolutionary feminist,' Sophia, Tekla, and Councillor Mikulin are admirably discerned and presented, and at the end Conrad's sense of scene, philosophy, and his deep,

[1] *Letters from Conrad*, p. 251.

reflective commentary on human vicissitudes all combine to convince us that this life was indeed such as he presents it.    The English have reason to be grateful for the great Russian novelists, Tolstoy, Turgenev, and Dostoevsky. *Under Western Eyes* obviously is a lesser peak, but it is a peak of the same range.

Of *The Mirror of the Sea* (1906) Conrad has defined his aim: [1]

I have tried with an almost filial regard to render the vibration of life in the great world of waters, in the hearts of the simple men who for ages have traversed its solitudes, and also that something sentient which seems to dwell in ships—the creatures of their hands and the objects of their care.

That he succeeded is shown by the tributes of Henry James, H. G. Wells, John Galsworthy, and E. V. Lucas, four authors whose testimony to Conrad's achievement must be cited here.    Henry James wrote, 1st November 1906:

But the book itself is a wonder to me really—for it's so bringing home the prodigy of your past experiences. . . . No one has *known*—for intellectual use—the things you know, and you have, as the artist of the whole matter, an authority that no one has approached. . . . Nothing you have done has more in it. The root of the matter of saying.    You stir me, in fine, to amazement and you touch me to tears, and I thank the powers who so mysteriously let you look with such sensibilities, into such an undiscovered country—for sensibility.

H. G. Wells wrote:

It's talk, good talk, discursive yet not without point, admirably expressive without at any time becoming deliberately and consciously eloquent, full of the wonderful calm, a quality that never deserts you.    A fine book . . . the sea under my eyes most wonderfully.    I shall for all my life be the wiser for it. I see better as I go to and fro.

[1] *Some Reminiscences*, p. 13.

Galsworthy, 30th September 1906:

*The Mirror of the Sea* is magnificent.   It ranks with your very
highest work, and I think the episode in *Initiation* the finest thing
you have written. . . . Your way of marshalling the stuff is
extraordinarily ingenious and repaying; and the book breathes a
single spirit—a loving spirit—out of its pages.   As I say, it is
the epic of the sailing ship.

E. V. Lucas wrote, 9th October 1906:

Your book has made me very sad—as all beautiful works of
art do.   It is so beautiful and so wise that I don't know what
to say about it.   I don't mind confessing that I cried a little as
I read it . . . you have made me so restless.   I don't know
what to do.   This tedious solid land. . . .

*Initiation* and *The Tremolino* are, as Galsworthy said, 'the
gems of the book,' and the latter is of autobiographical
value recording boldly and faithfully Conrad's early adventure in the Mediterranean as a Carlist gun-runner, with its
sketches of the seaman Dominic Cervoni, who was the
protype of Nostromo, and of Rita, who reappears later as
the heroine of *The Arrow of Gold*.   Generations of seamen
have passed, but no British writers have reproduced with
such justness and such delicate observation so many aspects
of the life of 'the simple men and the ships—the creatures
of their minds.'   The informality of 'the talks' is balanced
by their eloquence.   As Henry James put it: 'I read you as
I listen to rare music—with deepest depths of surrender,
and out of those depths I emerge slowly and reluctantly
again. . . .'   It is interesting to compare with this impression, Mr. Mégroz's verdict: '*The Mirror of the Sea* is a
little overcharged; it is like a row of pictures all equally
brilliant, or a speech in the sublime vein that is a little too
long.'   And one wonders whether this is not indicative of

the change in the circumstances and outlook of the younger
generation who have speeded up everything in life and have
no time for pictures or for eloquence.   The merchantmen
have passed.   Only the record of them in literature and art
remains.

The story of *The Tremolino* and its Mediterranean setting
sharply outlined and realistic brings up for discussion the
novel written twelve years later, *The Arrow of Gold* (1919),
where Conrad elaborated in fiction the romantic episode
which forty years earlier had led to his breaking abruptly
all his French connections and joining the English ship *The
Mavis* which brought him to Lowestoft, where he entered
on his new life with English seamen.   Galsworthy complained in letters to me: [1] 'I can find no real *feeling* in *The
Arrow of Gold* . . . *Youth* has glamour.   This hasn't a speck
of it . . . the spark left out'—a curious complaint, for
the book is alive with feeling, only not with the sharp
uprushing passionate feelings of romantic youth at twenty-
one.   Conrad explains in his preface:

> The subject . . . I had been carrying about with me for many
> years, not so much a possession of my memory as an inherent
> part of myself.   It was ever present to my mind and ready to
> my hand, but I was loth to touch it. . . . If I took it up so late
> in life it is because the right moment had not arrived till then.
> I mean the positive feeling of it, which is a thing that cannot
> be discussed.

It is certainly true that the book conveys a peculiar sense
that the reader is hearing the collaboration between a man
of twenty-one and his later self at sixty, and that the author
has not been able to draw the line sharply between what the
characters thought and did and said and his interpretations
and reflections and reasoning about them, so that the narra-

[1] *Letters from John Galsworthy*, pp. 235–6 (1934).

tive is at times overlaid with conjecture and comment; but despite this double outline, the novel as a work of art is none the less a *chef d'œuvre*.   The book is a lesson in the art of compression and abridgment, and of eliminating the in-essentials.   It is a lesson in the art of composition, of ordering and of developing the story with such *finesse* that we have no inkling of what is going to happen.   The art is very fine, too fine indeed for the ordinary reader, but the master has perfect command of his resources.   He is tanta-lizing, no doubt, like Rita, who keeps tantalizing M. George and eluding him, and M. George is also capricious and tantalizing, and too wilfully obdurate.   But the handling of the action is beyond praise, and when Sir Sidney Colvin warns us, 'let no one think he has really read this book until he has read it twice and it may be thrice, for the thrills and tension of the later development throw back with each reading a stronger reflected light on the introductory con-versations and bring out more clearly their artistic point and purposefulness,' [1] he is both truthful and a little naïve; for the early conversations ought to need no 'stronger re-flected light' to be thrown upon them later.   But if we admit that the conversations are often sophisticated, how intriguing is the drama, how masterly are the characters revealed, as Therese in her bigoted self-righteousness and peasant rapacity, and Ortega menacing and ridiculous with his lustful obsession for Rita, and Rita herself, the bewitch-ing heroine, and the Blunts, the impoverished Southern American aristocrats, both mother and son, with what decisive sharpness these people live in the memory.   How original is the ordering of the action, which culminates in the shattering *dénoûment*, strangely fantastic as life is when passions defy control.   While one does not agree with Sir

[1] Introduction to *The Arrow of Gold*, Collected Edition, p. x.

Sidney Colvin's verdict, 'it is in *The Arrow of Gold* that Conrad's genius shows itself at its highest power,' one can say that this flower of literary art, a little over-mature, reveals fresh unexpected contours of subtle beauty.

One might continue at length this running appreciation of Conrad's works and his enrichment of English literature by his portrayal of scenes and situations, and characters, shores and seas strange to it and unregistered; but the fact is that in all his best stories, such as *Falk*, *The End of the Tether*, *A Smile of Fortune*, *The Secret Sharer*, his creative vision opens up new vistas and emotional dramas, outside the radius of our insular perceptions and habits of thought. It is the creative vision that counts in the realm of records of the flesh and the spirit.    And the judgment of Conrad's fellow novelists as to his creative mastery, was emphatic. Thus we find Arnold Bennett's testimony in a letter of 22nd November 1912, from which we quote some extracts:

I read 'Higuerota' (*Nostromo*) again not long since. . . . When I first read it I thought it the finest novel of this generation (bar none), and I am still thinking so.    It is 'majestic and orbicular' and just peerless, and there's no more to be said.    It is the Higuerota among novels.    I was warned by an Ass that the latter half of *Under Western Eyes* was inferior to the beginning, and I have heard the opinion from others.    It is not true.    The whole book is superb. . . . Only other creative artists can understand a creative artist.    Which limits the public comprehension rather severely. . . . I wish I could acquaint you with my state of mind—intense satisfaction in seeing a thing truly done, mixed with anger because I know I can never do it as well myself —when I recall the quiet domestic scenes behind the shop in *The Secret Agent*, here is rather the sort of thing I reckon to handle myself—but I respectfully retire from the comparison. What I chiefly like in your books of *Reminiscences* is the increasing sardonic quality of them—the rich veins of dark and glittering satire and sarcasm. We want a lot more of that in English literature.

Conrad's reply to this letter must be quoted here as it explains as no other man's words could do, the long struggle he had carried on till then against ill-health and his unpopularity with the public:

The joy your praise of *Nostromo* has given me is immense. With the public it was the blackest possible frost. I was two years at it. It's true that one-third of that time was illness; but still it was a long effort. . . .

For myself, in my conscience, all I am aware of is a certain tenacity of purpose which has kept me going through these few years under mental and physical conditions of which I'll say nothing, as they were too intimately adverse to bear description. For the rest, I will only say that if the vintage be good, the merit of the bottle is slender. It just happened to hold it—that's all.

The clouds of unpopularity and financial worry were to break the next year, 1913, with the publication of *Chance*. As Hugh Walpole put it:

For twenty years the public had been told by the High Priests of literary taste that they must read Conrad and for twenty years the public had refused to listen. Now, for no reason of which it was aware, it changed its mind and Conrad was a popular novelist.

. . . Yes, this is the most English of all his books and it is pleasant to think that it was with this one that he won his popularity and the comfort of his later life. . . . The Fynes also are wonderful examples of Conrad's creative genius. This couple we might have sworn could be justly realized only by an English writer; any foreigner must caricature them from the very force of his wonder that such beings could exist. But the little Fynes and their dog are not caricatured at all; their goodness, their lack of imagination, the generosity that struggles with a sense of propriety, this is so English that we wonder whether Trollope could have done more finely.[1]

[1] *Chance*, Memorial Edition (1925). Introduction by Hugh Walpole.

If *Chance* be the most insular of Conrad's works, there is certainly something sardonically soothing in the fact that the British public was brought at long last to his feet by one of the least masterly of his novels. Not that it has not rare qualities, and many brilliant scenes, dramatic developments and great technical ingenuity [1]; but it has not the ease, certainty and inevitability in its artistic effect as a whole. However, Conrad tells us in his preface: 'in doing this book my intention was to interest people in my vision of things which is indissolubly allied to the style in which it is expressed.' And if there be too much of chance and circumstance conspiring to make the story, the English public loves to feel itself in the thick of the struggle with a great many things happening. So if the pattern of *Chance* be crowded and over intricate the foreign vision none the less is there prevailing with the English material.

We need not continue further our brief survey of Conrad's achievements. Enough has been said to show that English literature owes to Conrad an enrichment of our consciousness of human life that no British contemporary novelist could match and that he brought to our fiction a Slav psychological intensity of vision and feeling that was new to it. While he portrayed the life of English seamen with a realism and a romantic sense that no other writer has equalled, he drew the sea itself and its infinite moods with an atmospheric force and beauty that are magical in their illusion of reality. By his breadth of outlook, 'cosmic sense' of man's place in Nature, uncompromising sardonic perception of the human drama, by his subtle, ironic, generous-hearted spirit Conrad's creative temperament brought a new, foreign force into English Letters.

EDWARD GARNETT.

[1] See Edward Crankshaw's critical appreciation in *Joseph Conrad*, pp. 122-32 (1936).

# ALMAYER'S FOLLY

*Published in* 1895

# ALMAYER'S FOLLY

I am informed that in criticizing that literature which
preys on strange people and prowls in far-off countries,
under the shade of palms, in the unsheltered glare of
sunbeaten beaches, amongst honest cannibals and the more
sophisticated pioneers of our glorious virtues, a lady—
distinguished in the world of letters—summed up her
disapproval of it by saying that the tales it produced were
'decivilized.'   And in that sentence not only the tales
but, I apprehend, the strange people and the far-off
countries also, are finally condemned in a verdict of
contemptuous dislike.

A woman's judgment: intuitive, clever, expressed with
felicitous charm—infallible.   A judgment that has nothing
to do with justice.   The critic and the judge seems to
think that in those distant lands all joy is a yell and a war
dance, all pathos is a howl and a ghastly grin of filed
teeth, and that the solution of all problems is found in
the barrel of a revolver or on the point of an assegai.
And yet it is not so.   But the erring magistrate may
plead in excuse the misleading nature of the evidence.

The picture of life, there as here, is drawn with the
same elaboration of detail, coloured with the same tints.
Only in the cruel serenity of the sky, under the merciless
brilliance of the sun, the dazzled eye misses the delicate
detail, sees only the strong outlines, while the colours,
in the steady light, seem crude and without shadow.
Nevertheless it is the same picture.

And there is a bond between us and that humanity so
far away.   I am speaking here of men and women—not
of the charming and graceful phantoms that move about
in our mud and smoke and are softly luminous with the
radiance of all our virtues; that are possessed of all
refinements, of all sensibilities, of all wisdom—but, being
only phantoms, possess no heart.

The sympathies of those are (probably) with the
immortals: with the angels above or the devils below.
I am content to sympathize with common mortals, no
matter where they live; in houses or in tents, in the
streets under a fog, or in the forests behind the dark
line of dismal mangroves that fringe the vast solitude of
the sea.   For, their land—like ours—lies under the inscrutable eyes of the Most High.   Their hearts—like
ours—must endure the load of the gifts from Heaven: the
curse of facts and the blessing of illusions, the bitterness of
our wisdom and the deceptive consolation of our folly.

1895.                                                                    J. C.

# AN OUTCAST
# OF THE ISLANDS

*Published in* 1896

# AN OUTCAST OF THE ISLANDS

*An Outcast of the Islands* is my second novel in the absolute sense of the word; second in conception, second in execution, second as it were in its essence. There was no hesitation, half-formed plan, vague idea, or the vaguest reverie of anything else between it and *Almayer's Folly*. The only doubt I suffered from, after the publication of *Almayer's Folly*, was whether I should write another line for print. Those days, now grown so dim, had their poignant moments. Neither in my mind nor in my heart had I then given up the sea. In truth I was clinging to it desperately, all the more desperately because, against my will, I could not help feeling that there was something changed in my relation to it. *Almayer's Folly* had been finished and done with. The mood itself was gone. But it had left the memory of an experience that, both in thought and emotion, was unconnected with the sea, and I suppose that part of my moral being which is rooted in consistency was badly shaken. I was a victim of contrary stresses which produced a state of immobility. I gave myself up to indolence. Since it was impossible for me to face both ways I had elected to face nothing. The discovery of new values in life is a very chaotic experience; there is a tremendous amount of jostling and confusion and a momentary feeling of darkness. I let my spirit float supine over that chaos.

A phrase of Edward Garnett's is, as a matter of fact, responsible for this book. The first of the friends I made for myself by my pen, it was but natural that he should be the recipient, at that time, of my confidences. One evening when we had dined together and he had listened to the account of my perplexities (I fear he must have been growing a little tired of them) he pointed out that there was no need to determine my future absolutely. Then he added: 'You have the style, you have the temperament; why not write another?' I believe that as far as one man may wish to influence another man's life Edward Garnett had a great desire that I should go on writing. At that time, and, I may say, ever afterwards, he was always very patient and gentle with me. What strikes me most, however, in the phrase quoted above which was offered to me in a tone of detachment is not its gentleness but its effective wisdom. Had he said, 'Why not go on writing?' it is very probable he would have scared me away from pen and ink for ever; but there was nothing either to frighten one or arouse one's antagonism in the mere suggestion to 'write another.' And thus a dead point in the revolution of my affairs was insidiously got over. The word 'another' did it. At about eleven o'clock of a nice London night, Edward and I walked along interminable streets talking of many things, and I remember that on getting home I sat down and wrote about half a page of *An Outcast of the Islands* before I slept. This was committing myself definitely, I won't say to another life, but to another book. There is apparently something in my character which will not allow me to abandon for good any piece of work I have begun. I have laid aside many beginnings. I have laid them aside with sorrow, with disgust, with rage, with melancholy, and even with self-contempt; but even at the worst I had an uneasy consciousness that I would have to go back to them.

*An Outcast of the Islands* belongs to those novels of mine that were never laid aside; and though it brought me the qualification of 'exotic writer' I don't think the charge was at all justified. For the life of me I don't see that there is the slightest exotic spirit in the conception or style of that novel. It is certainly the most *tropical* of my eastern tales. The mere scenery got a great hold on me as I went on, perhaps because (I may just as well confess that) the story itself was never very near my heart. It engaged my imagination much more than my affection. As to my feeling for Willems it was but the regard one cannot help having for one's own creation. Obviously I could not be indifferent to a man on whose head I had brought so much evil simply by imagining him such as he appears in the novel—and that, too, on a very slight foundation.

The man who suggested Willems to me was not particularly interesting in himself. My interest was aroused by his dependent position, his strange, dubious status of a mistrusted, disliked, worn-out European living on the reluctant toleration of that settlement hidden in the heart of the forest-land, up that sombre stream which our ship was the only white men's ship to visit. With his hollow, clean-shaved cheeks, a heavy grey moustache and eyes without any expression whatever, clad always in a spotless sleeping suit much befrogged in front, which left his lean neck wholly uncovered, and with his bare feet in a pair of straw slippers, he wandered silently amongst the houses in daylight, almost as dumb as an animal and apparently much more homeless. I don't know what he did with himself at night. He must have had a place, a hut, a palm-leaf shed, some sort of hovel where he kept his razor and his change of sleeping suits. An air of futile mystery hung over him, something not exactly dark but obviously ugly. The only definite statement I could extract from anybody was that it was he who had 'brought the Arabs into the river.' That must have happened many years before. But how did he bring them into the river? He could hardly have done it in his arms like a lot of kittens. I knew that Almayer founded the chronology of all his misfortunes on the date of that fateful advent; and yet the very first time we dined with Almayer there was Willems sitting at table with us in the manner of the skeleton at the feast, obviously shunned by everybody, never addressed by any one, and for all recognition of his existence getting now and then from Almayer a venomous glance which I observed with great surprise. In the course of the whole evening he ventured one single remark which I didn't catch because his articulation was imperfect, as of a man who had forgotten how to speak. I was the only person who seemed aware of the sound. Willems subsided. Presently he retired, pointedly un-noticed—into the forest maybe? Its immensity was there, within three hundred yards of the veranda, ready to swallow up anything. Almayer, conversing with my captain, did not stop talking while he glared angrily at the retreating back. Didn't that fellow bring the Arabs into the river! Nevertheless Willems turned up next morning on Almayer's veranda. From the bridge of the steamer I could see plainly these two, breakfasting together, *tête-à-tête* and, I suppose, in dead silence, one with his air of being no longer interested in this world and the other raising his eyes now and then with intense dislike.

It was clear that in those days Willems lived on Almayer's charity. Yet on returning two months later to Sambir I heard that he had gone on an expedition up the river in charge of a steam-launch belonging to the Arabs, to make some discovery or other. On account of the strange reluctance that every one manifested to talk about Willems it was impossible for me to get at the rights of that transaction. Moreover, I was a new-comer, the youngest of the company, and, I suspect, not judged quite fit as yet for a full confidence. I was not much concerned about that exclusion. The faint suggestion of plots and mysteries pertaining to all matters touching Almayer's affairs amused me vastly. Almayer was obviously very much affected. I believe he missed Willems immensely. He wore an air of sinister preoccupation and talked confidentially with my captain. I could catch only snatches of mumbled sentences. Then one morning as I came along the deck to take my place at the breakfast table Almayer checked himself in his low-toned discourse. My captain's face was perfectly impenetrable. There was a moment of profound silence and then as if unable to contain himself Almayer burst out in a loud, vicious tone:

'One thing's certain; if he finds anything worth having up there they will poison him like a dog.'

Disconnected though it was, that phrase, as food for thought, was distinctly worth hearing. We left the river three days afterwards and I never returned to Sambir; but whatever happened to the protagonist of my Willems nobody can deny that I have recorded for him a less squalid fate.

1919.                                          J. C.

# THE NIGGER OF THE 'NARCISSUS'

## A Tale of the Sea

*Published in* 1897

# THE NIGGER OF THE 'NARCISSUS'

A work that aspires, however humbly, to the condition of art should carry its justification in every line. And art itself may be defined as a single-minded attempt to render the highest kind of justice to the visible universe, by bringing to light the truth, manifold and one, under-lying its every aspect. It is an attempt to find in its forms, in its colours, in its light, in its shadows, in the aspects of matter, and in the facts of life what of each is fundamental, what is enduring and essential—their one illuminating and convincing quality—the very truth of their existence. The artist, then, like the thinker or the scientist, seeks the truth and makes his appeal. Impressed by the aspect of the world the thinker plunges into ideas, the scientist into facts—whence, presently, emerging they make their appeal to those qualities of our being that fit us best for the hazardous enterprise of living. They speak authoritatively to our common sense, to our intelligence, to our desire of peace, or to our desire of unrest; not seldom to our prejudices, sometimes to our fears, often to our egoism—but always to our credulity. And their words are heard with reverence, for their concern is with weighty matters: with the cultivation of our minds and the proper care of our bodies, with the attainment of our ambitions, with the perfection of the means and the glorification of our precious aims.

It is otherwise with the artist.

Confronted by the same enigmatical spectacle the artist

descends within himself, and in that lonely region of stress
and strife, if he be deserving and fortunate, he finds the
terms of his appeal.    His appeal is made to our less
obvious capacities: to that part of our nature which,
because of the warlike conditions of existence, is necessarily kept out of sight within the more resisting and hard
qualities—like the vulnerable body within a steel armour.
His appeal is less loud, more profound, less distinct, more
stirring—and sooner forgotten.    Yet its effect endures
for ever.    The changing wisdom of successive generations
discards ideas, questions facts, demolishes theories.    But
the artist appeals to that part of our being which is not
dependent on wisdom; to that in us which is a gift and
not an acquisition—and, therefore, more permanently
enduring.    He speaks to our capacity for delight and
wonder, to the sense of mystery surrounding our lives;
to our sense of pity, and beauty, and pain; to the latent
feeling of fellowship with all creation—and to the subtle
but invincible conviction of solidarity that knits together
the loneliness of innumerable hearts, to the solidarity in
dreams, in joy, in sorrow, in aspirations, in illusions, in
hope, in fear, which binds men to each other, which binds
together all humanity—the dead to the living and the
living to the unborn.

It is only some such train of thought, or rather of
feeling, that can in a measure explain the aim of the
attempt, made in the tale which follows, to present an
unrestful episode in the obscure lives of a few individuals
out of all the disregarded multitude of the bewildered,
the simple, and the voiceless.    For, if any part of truth
dwells in the belief confessed above, it becomes evident
that there is not a place of splendour or a dark corner of

the earth that does not deserve, if only a passing glance
of wonder and pity.  The motive, then, may be held to
justify the matter of the work; but this preface, which
is simply an avowal of endeavour, cannot end here—for
the avowal is not yet complete.

Fiction—if it at all aspires to be art—appeals to temperament.  And in truth it must be, like painting, like
music, like all art, the appeal of one temperament to all
the other innumerable temperaments whose subtle and
resistless power endows passing events with their true
meaning, and creates the moral, the emotional atmosphere
of the place and time.  Such an appeal to be effective
must be an impression conveyed through the senses; and,
in fact, it cannot be made in any other way, because
temperament, whether individual or collective, is not
amenable to persuasion.  All art, therefore, appeals
primarily to the senses, and the artistic aim when expressing itself in written words must also make its appeal
through the senses, if its high desire is to reach the secret
spring of responsive emotions. It must strenuously aspire to
the plasticity of sculpture, to the colour of painting, and to
the magic suggestiveness of music—which is the art of arts.
And it is only through complete, unswerving devotion to
the perfect blending of form and substance; it is only through
an unremitting never-discouraged care for the shape and
ring of sentences that an approach can be made to plasticity,
to colour, and that the light of magic suggestiveness may be
brought to play for an evanescent instant over the commonplace surface of words: of the old, old words, worn thin,
defaced by ages of careless usage.

The sincere endeavour to accomplish that creative task,
to go as far on that road as his strength will carry him, to

go undeterred by faltering, weariness, or reproach, is the
only valid justification for the worker in prose.  And if
his conscience is clear, his answer to those who, in the
fullness of a wisdom which looks for immediate profit,
demand specifically to be edified, consoled, amused; who
demand to be promptly improved, or encouraged, or
frightened, or shocked, or charmed, must run thus:
My task which I am trying to achieve is, by the power
of the written word to make you hear, to make you feel
—it is, before all, to make you *see*.  That—and no more,
and it is everything.  If I succeed, you shall find there
according to your deserts: encouragement, consolation,
fear, charm—all you demand—and, perhaps, also that
glimpse of truth for which you have forgotten to ask.

To snatch in a moment of courage, from the remorseless rush of time, a passing phase of life, is only the
beginning of the task.  The task approached in tenderness and faith is to hold up unquestioningly, without
choice and without fear, the rescued fragment before all
eyes in the light of a sincere mood.  It is to show its
vibration, its colour, its form; and through its movement, its form, and its colour, reveal the substance of
its truth—disclose its inspiring secret: the stress and
passion within the core of each convincing moment.  In
a single-minded attempt of that kind, if one be deserving
and fortunate, one may perchance attain to such clearness
of sincerity that at last the presented vision of regret or
pity, of terror or mirth, shall awaken in the hearts of
the beholders that feeling of unavoidable solidarity; of the
solidarity in mysterious origin, in toil, in joy, in hope,
in uncertain fate, which binds men to each other and all
mankind to the visible world.

It is evident that he who, rightly or wrongly, holds by the convictions expressed above cannot be faithful to any one of the temporary formulas of his craft. The enduring part of them—the truth which each only imperfectly veils—should abide with him as the most precious of his possessions, but they all: Realism, Romanticism, Naturalism, even the unofficial sentimentalism (which, like the poor, is exceedingly difficult to get rid of), all these gods must, after a short period of fellowship, abandon him—even on the very threshold of the temple —to the stammerings of his conscience and to the outspoken consciousness of the difficulties of his work. In that uneasy solitude the supreme cry of Art for Art, itself, loses the exciting ring of its apparent immorality. It sounds far off. It has ceased to be a cry, and is heard only as a whisper, often incomprehensible, but at times and faintly encouraging.

Sometimes, stretched at ease in the shade of a roadside tree, we watch the motions of a labourer in a distant field, and after a time, begin to wonder languidly as to what the fellow may be at. We watch the movements of his body, the waving of his arms, we see him bend down, stand up, hesitate, begin again. It may add to the charm of an idle hour to be told the purpose of his exertions. If we know he is trying to lift a stone, to dig a ditch, to uproot a stump, we look with a more real interest at his efforts; we are disposed to condone the jar of his agitation upon the restfulness of the landscape; and even, if in a brotherly frame of mind, we may bring ourselves to forgive his failure. We understood his object, and, after all, the fellow has tried, and perhaps he had not the strength—and perhaps he had not the knowledge. We forgive, go on our way—and forget.

And so it is with the workman of art. Art is long and life is short, and success is very far off. And thus, doubtful of strength to travel so far, we talk a little about the aim—the aim of art, which, like life itself, is inspiring, difficult—obscured by mists. It is not in the clear logic of a triumphant conclusion; it is not in the unveiling of one of those heartless secrets which are called the Laws of Nature. It is not less great, but only more difficult.

To arrest, for the space of a breath, the hands busy about the work of the earth, and compel men entranced by the sight of distant goals to glance for a moment at the surrounding vision of form and colour, of sunshine and shadows; to make them pause for a look, for a sigh, for a smile—such is the aim, difficult and evanescent, and reserved only for a very few to achieve. But sometimes, by the deserving and the fortunate, even that task is accomplished. And when it is accomplished—behold!—all the truth of life is there: a moment of vision, a sigh, a smile—and the return to an eternal rest.

1897.                                              J. C.

# TALES OF UNREST

Karain: A Memory
The Idiots
An Outpost of Progress
The Return
The Lagoon

*Published in* 1898

# TALES OF UNREST

Of the five stories in this volume *The Lagoon*, the last in order, is the earliest in date. It is the first short story I ever wrote and marks, in a manner of speaking, the end of my first phase, the Malayan phase with its special subject and its verbal suggestions. Conceived in the same mood which produced *Almayer's Folly* and *An Outcast of the Islands*, it is told in the same breath (with what was left of it, that is, after the end of *An Outcast*), seen with the same vision, rendered in the same method —if such a thing as method did exist then in my conscious relation to this new adventure of writing for print. I doubt it very much. One does one's work first and theorizes about it afterwards. It is a very amusing and egotistical occupation of no use whatever to any one and just as likely as not to lead to false conclusions.

Anybody can see that between the last paragraph of *An Outcast* and the first of *The Lagoon* there has been no change of pen, figuratively speaking. It happens also to be literally true. It was the same pen: a common steel pen. Having been charged with a certain lack of emotional faculty I am glad to be able to say that on one occasion at least I did give way to a sentimental impulse. I thought the pen had been a good pen and that it had done enough for me, and so, with the idea of keeping it for a sort of memento on which I could look later with tender eyes, I put it into my waistcoat pocket. Afterwards it used to turn up in all sorts of places, at the bottom of small drawers, among my studs in cardboard boxes, till at last it found permanent rest in a large wooden bowl containing some loose keys, bits of sealing-wax, bits of string, small broken chains, a few buttons, and similar minute wreckage that washes out of a man's life into such receptacles. I would catch sight of it from time to time with a distinct feeling of satisfaction till, one day, I perceived with horror that there were two old pens in there. How the other pen found its way into the bowl instead of the fire-place or wastepaper basket I can't imagine, but there the two were, lying side by side, both encrusted with ink and completely undistinguishable from each other. It was very distressing, but being determined not to share my sentiment between two pens or run the risk of sentimentalizing over a mere stranger, I threw them both out of the window into a flower-bed —which strikes me now as a poetical grave for the remnants of one's past.

But the tale remained. It was first fixed in print in the *Cornhill Magazine*, being my first appearance in a serial of any kind; and I have lived long enough to see it most agreeably guyed by Mr. Max Beerbohm in a volume of parodies entitled *A Christmas Garland*, where I found myself in very good company. I was immensely gratified. I began to believe in my public existence. I have much to thank *The Lagoon* for.

My next effort in short story writing was a departure —I mean a departure from the Malay Archipelago. Without premeditation, without sorrow, without rejoicing, and almost without noticing it, I stepped into the very different atmosphere of *An Outpost of Progress*. I found there a different moral attitude. I seemed able to capture new

reactions, new suggestions, and even new rhythms for my
paragraphs. For a moment I fancied myself a new man
—a most exciting illusion. It clung to me for some time,
monstrous, half conviction and half hope as to its body,
with an iridescent tail of dreams and with a changeable
head like a plastic mask. It was only later that I perceived
that in common with the rest of men nothing could
deliver me from my fatal consistency. We cannot escape
from ourselves.

An Outpost of Progress is the lightest part of the
loot I carried off from Central Africa, the main portion
being of course the Heart of Darkness. Other men
have found a lot of quite different things there and I have
the comfortable conviction that what I took would not
have been of much use to anybody else. And it must
be said that it was but a very small amount of plunder.
All of it could go into one's breast pocket when folded
neatly. As for the story itself it is true enough in its
essentials. The sustained invention of a really telling lie
demands a talent which I do not possess.

'The Idiots' is such an obviously derivative piece of
work that it is impossible for me to say anything about
it here. The suggestion of it was not mental but visual:
the actual idiots. It was after an interval of long groping
amongst vague impulses and hesitations which ended in
the production of The Nigger that I turned to my third
short story in the order of time, the first in this volume:
Karain: A Memory.

Reading it after many years Karain produced on me
the effect of something seen through a pair of glasses
from a rather advantageous position. In that story I had
not gone back to the Archipelago, I had only turned for

another look at it. I admit that I was absorbed by the distant view, so absorbed that I didn't notice then that the *motif* of the story is almost identical with the *motif* of *The Lagoon*. However, the idea at the back is very different; but the story is mainly made memorable to me by the fact that it was my first contribution to *Blackwood's Magazine* and that it led to my personal acquaintance with Mr. William Blackwood, whose guarded appreciation I felt nevertheless to be genuine, and prized accordingly. *Karain* was begun on a sudden impulse only three days after I wrote the last line of *The Nigger*, and the recollection of its difficulties is mixed up with the worries of the unfinished *Return*, the last pages of which I took up again at the time; the only instance in my life when I made an attempt to write with both hands at once as it were.

Indeed my innermost feeling, now, is that *The Return* is a left-handed production. Looking through that story lately I had the material impression of sitting under a large and expensive umbrella in the loud drumming of a furious rain-shower. It was very distracting. In the general uproar one could hear every individual drop strike on the stout and distended silk. Mentally, the reading rendered me dumb for the remainder of the day, not exactly with astonishment but with a sort of dismal wonder. I don't want to talk disrespectfully of any pages of mine. Psychologically there were no doubt good reasons for my attempt; and it was worth while, if only to see of what excesses I was capable in that sort of virtuosity. In this connection I should like to confess my surprise on finding that notwithstanding all its apparatus of analysis the story consists for the most part of physical impressions; impressions of sound and sight, railway station, streets, a trotting horse, reflections in mirrors, and so on, rendered as if for their own sake and combined with a sublimated description of a desirable middle class town-residence which somehow manages to produce a sinister effect. For the rest any kind word about *The Return* (and there have been such words said at different times) awakens in me the liveliest gratitude, for I know how much the writing of that fantasy has cost me in sheer toil, in temper, and in disillusion.

J. C.

# LORD JIM

## A Tale

*Published in* 1900

# LORD JIM

When this novel first appeared in book form a notion got about that I had been bolted away with. Some reviewers maintained that the work starting as a short story had got beyond the writer's control. One or two discovered internal evidence of the fact, which seemed to amuse them. They pointed out the limitations of the narrative form. They argued that no man could have been expected to talk all that time, and other men to listen so long. It was not, they said, very credible.

After thinking it over for something like sixteen years I am not so sure about that. Men have been known, both in the tropics and in the temperate zone, to sit up half the night 'swapping yarns.' This, however, is but one yarn, yet with interruptions affording some measure of relief; and in regard to the listeners' endurance, the postulate must be accepted that the story *was* interesting. It is the necessary preliminary assumption. If I hadn't believed that it *was* interesting I could never have begun to write it. As to the mere physical possibility we all know that some speeches in Parliament have taken nearer six than three hours in delivery; whereas all that part of the book which is Marlow's narrative can be read through aloud, I should say, in less than three hours. Besides— though I have kept strictly all such insignificant details out of the tale—we may presume that there must have been refreshments on that night, a glass of mineral water of some sort to help the narrator on.

But, seriously, the truth of the matter is, that my first thought was of a short story, concerned only with the pilgrim ship episode; nothing more. And that was a legitimate conception. After writing a few pages, however, I became for some reason discontented and I laid them aside for a time. I didn't take them out of the drawer till the late Mr. William Blackwood suggested I should give something again to his magazine.

It was only then that I perceived that the pilgrim ship episode was a good starting-point for a free and wandering tale; that it was an event, too, which could conceivably colour the whole 'sentiment of existence' in a simple and sensitive character. But all these preliminary moods and stirrings of spirit were rather obscure at the time, and they do not appear clearer to me now after the lapse of so many years.

The few pages I had laid aside were not without their weight in the choice of subject. But the whole was re-written deliberately. When I sat down to it I knew it would be a long book, though I didn't foresee that it would spread itself over thirteen numbers of *Maga*.

I have been asked at times whether this was not the book of mine I liked best. I am a great foe to favouritism in public life, in private life, and even in the delicate relationship of an author to his works. As a matter of principle I will have no favourites; but I don't go so far as to feel grieved and annoyed by the preference some people give to my Lord Jim. I won't even say that I 'fail to understand. . . .' No! But once I had occasion to be puzzled and surprised.

A friend of mine returning from Italy had talked with a lady there who did not like the book. I regretted that, of course, but what surprised me was the ground of her dislike.  'You know,' she said, 'it is all so morbid.'

The pronouncement gave me food for an hour's anxious thought.  Finally I arrived at the conclusion that, making due allowances for the subject itself being rather foreign to women's normal sensibilities, the lady could not have been an Italian.  I wonder whether she was European at all ?  In any case, no Latin temperament would have perceived anything morbid in the acute consciousness of lost honour.  Such a consciousness may be wrong, or it may be right, or it may be condemned as artificial; and, perhaps, my Jim is not a type of wide commonness.  But I can safely assure my readers that he is not the product of coldly perverted thinking.  He 's not a figure of northern mists either.  One sunny morning in the commonplace surroundings of an eastern roadstead, I saw his form pass by — appealing — significant — under a cloud — perfectly silent.  Which is as it should be.  It was for me, with all the sympathy of which I was capable, to seek fit words for his meaning.  He was 'one of us.'

*June 1917.*                                    J. C.

# YOUTH

## A Narrative and Two Other Stories

Heart of Darkness
The End of the Tether

*Published in* 1902

# YOUTH

The three stories in this volume lay no claim to unity of artistic purpose. The only bond between them is that of the time in which they were written. They belong to the period immediately following the publication of *The Nigger of the 'Narcissus,'* and preceding the first conception of *Nostromo*, two books which, it seems to me, stand apart and by themselves in the body of my work. It is also the period during which I contributed to *Maga*; a period dominated by *Lord Jim* and associated in my grateful memory with the late Mr. William Blackwood's encouraging and helpful kindness.

*Youth* was not my first contribution to *Maga*. It was the second. But that story marks the first appearance in the world of the man Marlow, with whom my relations have grown very intimate in the course of years. The origins of that gentleman (nobody as far as I know had ever hinted that he was anything but that)—his origins have been the subject of some literary speculation of, I am glad to say, a friendly nature.

One would think that I am the proper person to throw a light on the matter; but in truth I find that it isn't so easy. It is pleasant to remember that nobody had charged him with fraudulent purposes or looked down on him as a charlatan; but apart from that he was supposed to be all sorts of things: a clever screen, a mere device, a 'personator,' a familiar spirit, a whispering 'daemon.' I myself have been suspected of a meditated plan for his capture.

F

That is not so. I made no plans. The man Marlow and I came together in the casual manner of those health-resort acquaintances which sometimes ripen into friend-ships. This one has ripened. For all his assertiveness in matters of opinion he is not an intrusive person. He haunts my hours of solitude, when, in silence, we lay our heads together in great comfort and harmony; but as we part at the end of a tale I am never sure that it may not be for the last time. Yet I don't think that either of us would care much to survive the other. In his case, at any rate, his occupation would be gone and he would suffer from that extinction, because I suspect him of some vanity. I don't mean vanity in the Solomonian sense. Of all my people he's the one that has never been a vexation to my spirit. A most discreet, understanding man. . . .

Even before appearing in book-form *Youth* was very well received. It lies on me to confess at last, and this is as good a place for it as another, that I have been all my life—all my two lives—the spoiled adopted child of Great Britain and even of the Empire; for it was Australia that gave me my first command. I break out into this declaration not because of a lurking tendency to megalo-mania, but, on the contrary, as a man who has no very notable illusions about himself. I follow the instincts of vain-glory and humility natural to all mankind. For it can hardly be denied that it is not their own deserts that men are most proud of, but rather of their prodigious luck, of their marvellous fortune: of that in their lives for which thanks and sacrifices must be offered on the altars of the inscrutable gods.

*Heart of Darkness* also received a certain amount of

notice from the first; and of its origins this much may be
said: it is well known that curious men go prying into all
sorts of places (where they have no business) and come out
of them with all kinds of spoil. This story, and one other,
not in this volume, are all the spoil I brought out from the
centre of Africa, where, really, I had no sort of business.
More ambitious in its scope and longer in the telling,
*Heart of Darkness* is quite as authentic in fundamentals
as *Youth*. It is, obviously, written in another mood,
I won't characterize the mood precisely, but anybody can
see that it is anything but the mood of wistful regret, of
reminiscent tenderness.

One more remark may be added. *Youth* is a feat of
memory. It is a record of experience; but that experience, in its facts, in its inwardness and in its outward colouring, begins and ends in myself. *Heart of
Darkness* is experience, too, but it is experience pushed
a little (and only very little) beyond the actual facts of
the case for the perfectly legitimate, I believe, purpose of
bringing it home to the minds and bosoms of the readers.
There it was no longer a matter of sincere colouring. It
was like another art altogether. That sombre theme
had to be given a sinister resonance, a tonality of its
own, a continued vibration that, I hoped, would hang in
the air and dwell on the ear after the last note had been
struck.

After saying so much there remains the last tale of the
book, still untouched. *The End of the Tether* is a
story of sea-life in a rather special way; and the most
intimate thing I can say of it is this: that having lived
that life fully, amongst its men, its thoughts and sensations,
I have found it possible, without the slightest misgiving,

in all sincerity of heart and peace of conscience, to con-
ceive the existence of Captain Whalley's personality and
to relate the manner of his end.　This statement acquires
some force from the circumstance that the pages of that
story—a fair half of the book—are also the product of
experience.　That experience belongs (like *Youth's*) to
the time before I ever thought of putting pen to paper.
As to its 'reality,' that is for the readers to determine.
One had to pick up one's facts here and there.　More
skill would have made them more real and the whole
composition more interesting.　But here we are approaching the veiled region of artistic values which it would be
improper and indeed dangerous for me to enter.　I have
looked over the proofs, have corrected a misprint or
two, have changed a word or two—and that 's all.　It is
not very likely that I shall ever read *The End of the
Tether* again.　No more need be said.　It accords best
with my feelings to part from Captain Whalley in
affectionate silence.

1917.　　　　　　　　　　　　　　　　　　J. C.

# TYPHOON

## And Other Stories

Amy Foster
Falk: A Reminiscence
To-morrow

*Published in* 1903

# TYPHOON

The main characteristic of this volume consists in this, that all the stories composing it belong not only to the same period but have been written one after another in the order in which they appear in the book.

The period is that which follows on my connection with *Blackwood's Magazine*. I had just finished writing *The End of the Tether* and was casting about for some subject which could be developed in a shorter form than the tales in the volume of *Youth* when the instance of a steamship full of returning coolies from Singapore to some port in northern China occurred to my recollection. Years before I had heard it being talked about in the East as a recent occurrence. It was for us merely one subject of conversation amongst many others of the kind. Men earning their bread in any very specialized occupation will talk shop, not only because it is the most vital interest of their lives but also because they have not much knowledge of other subjects. They have never had the time to get acquainted with them. Life, for most of us, is not so much a hard as an exacting taskmaster.

I never met anybody personally concerned in this affair, the interest of which for us was, of course, not the bad weather but the extraordinary complication brought into the ship's life at a moment of exceptional stress by the human element below her deck. Neither was the story itself ever enlarged upon in my hearing. In that company each of us could imagine easily what the whole thing was like. The financial difficulty of it, presenting also a human problem, was solved by a mind much too simple to be perplexed by anything in the world except men's idle talk for which it was not adapted.

From the first the mere anecdote, the mere statement I might say, that such a thing had happened on the high seas, appeared to me a sufficient subject for meditation. Yet it was but a bit of a sea yarn after all. I felt that to bring out its deeper significance which was quite apparent to me, something other, something more was required; a leading motive that would harmonize all these violent noises, and a point of view that would put all that elemental fury into its proper place.

What was needed of course was Captain MacWhirr. Directly I perceived him I could see that he was the man for the situation. I don't mean to say that I ever saw Captain MacWhirr in the flesh, or had ever come in contact with his literal mind and his dauntless temperament. MacWhirr is not an acquaintance of a few hours, or a few weeks, or a few months. He is the product of twenty years of life. My own life. Conscious invention had little to do with him. If it is true that Captain MacWhirr never walked and breathed on this earth (which I find for my part extremely difficult to believe) I can also assure my readers that he is perfectly authentic. I may venture to assert the same of every aspect of the story, while I confess that the particular typhoon of the tale was not a typhoon of my actual experience.

At its first appearance *Typhoon*, the story, was classed by some critics as a deliberately intended storm-piece. Others picked out MacWhirr, in whom they perceived a definite symbolic intention. Neither was exclusively my intention. Both the typhoon and Captain MacWhirr presented themselves to me as the necessities of the deep conviction with which I approached the subject of the story. It was their opportunity. It was also my opportunity; and it would be vain to discourse about what I made of it in a handful of pages, since the pages themselves are here, between the covers of this volume, to speak for themselves.

This is a belated reflection. If it had occurred to me before it would have perhaps done away with the existence of this Author's Note; for, indeed, the same remark applies to every story in this volume. None of them are stories of experience in the absolute sense of the word. Experience in them is but the canvas of the attempted picture. Each of them has its more than one intention. With each the question is what the writer has done with his opportunity; and each answers the question for itself in words which, if I may say so without undue solemnity, were written with a conscientious regard for the truth of my own sensations. And each of those stories, to mean something, must justify itself in its own way to the conscience of each successive reader.

Falk—the second story in the volume—offended the delicacy of one critic at least by certain peculiarities of its subject. But what is the subject of Falk? I personally do not feel so very certain about it. He who reads must find out for himself. My intention in writing Falk was not to shock anybody. As in most of my writings I insist not on the events but on their effect upon the persons in the tale. But in everything I have written there is always one invariable intention, and that is to capture the reader's attention, by securing his interest and enlisting his sympathies for the matter in hand, whatever it may be, within the limits of the visible world and within the boundaries of human emotions.

I may safely say that Falk is absolutely true to my experience of certain straightforward characters combining a perfectly natural ruthlessness with a certain amount of moral delicacy. Falk obeys the law of self-preservation without the slightest misgivings as to his right, but at a crucial turn of that ruthlessly preserved life he will not condescend to dodge the truth. As he is presented as sensitive enough to be affected permanently by a certain unusual experience, that experience had to be set by me before the reader vividly; but it is not the subject of the tale. If we go by mere facts then the subject is Falk's attempt to get married; in which the narrator of the tale finds himself unexpectedly involved both on its ruthless and its delicate side.

*Falk* shares with one other of my stories (*The Return* in the *Tales of Unrest* volume) the distinction of never having been serialized. I think the copy was shown to the editor of some magazine who rejected it indignantly on the sole ground that 'the girl never says anything.' This is perfectly true. From first to last Hermann's niece utters no word in the tale—and it is not because she is dumb, but for the simple reason that whenever she happens to come under the observation of the narrator she has either no occasion or is too profoundly moved to speak. The editor, who obviously had read the story, might have perceived that for himself. Apparently he did not, and I refrained from pointing out the impossibility to him because, since he did not venture to say that 'the girl' did not live, I felt no concern at his indignation.

All the other stories were serialized. The *Typhoon* appeared in the early numbers of the *Pall Mall Magazine*, then under the direction of the late Mr. Halkett. It was on that occasion, too, that I saw for the first time my conceptions rendered by an artist in another medium. Mr. Maurice Greiffenhagen knew how to combine in his illustrations the effect of his own most distinguished personal vision with an absolute fidelity to the inspiration of the writer. *Amy Foster* was published in the *Illustrated London News* with a fine drawing of Amy on her day out giving tea to the children at her home, in a hat with a big feather. *To-morrow* appeared first in the *Pall Mall Magazine*. Of that story I will only say that it struck many people by its adaptability to the stage and that I was induced to dramatize it under the title of *One Day More*; up to the present my only effort in that direction. I may also add that each of the four stories on their appearance in book form was picked out on various grounds as the 'best of the lot' by different critics, who reviewed the volume with a warmth of appreciation and understanding, a sympathetic insight, and a friendliness of expression for which I cannot be sufficiently grateful.

1919.                                          J. C.

# NOSTROMO

A Tale of the Seaboard

*Published in* 1904

# NOSTROMO

*Nostromo* is the most anxiously meditated of the longer novels which belong to the period following upon the publication of the *Typhoon* volume of short stories.

I don't mean to say that I became then conscious of any impending change in my mentality and in my attitude towards the tasks of my writing life. And perhaps there was never any change, except in that mysterious, extraneous thing which has nothing to do with the theories of art; a subtle change in the nature of the inspiration; a phenomenon for which I cannot in any way be held responsible. What, however, did cause me some concern was that after finishing the last story of the *Typhoon* volume it seemed somehow that there was nothing more in the world to write about.

This so strangely negative but disturbing mood lasted some little time; and then, as with many of my longer stories, the first hint for *Nostromo* came to me in the shape of a vagrant anecdote completely destitute of valuable details.

As a matter of fact in 1875 or '6, when very young, in the West Indies, or rather in the Gulf of Mexico, for my contacts with land were short, few, and fleeting, I heard the story of some man who was supposed to have stolen single-handed a whole lighter-full of silver, somewhere on the Tierra Firme seaboard during the troubles of a revolution.

On the face of it this was something of a feat. But

I heard no details, and having no particular interest in crime *qua* crime I was not likely to keep that one in my mind. And I forgot it till twenty-six or seven years afterwards I came upon the very thing in a shabby volume picked up outside a second-hand bookshop. It was the life story of an American seaman written by himself with the assistance of a journalist. In the course of his wanderings that American sailor worked for some months on board a schooner, the master and owner of which was the thief of whom I had heard in my very young days. I have no doubt of that because there could hardly have been two exploits of that peculiar kind in the same part of the world and both connected with a South American revolution.

The fellow had actually managed to steal a lighter with silver, and this, it seems, only because he was implicitly trusted by his employers, who must have been singularly poor judges of character. In the sailor's story he is represented as an unmitigated rascal, a small cheat, stupidly ferocious, morose, of mean appearance, and altogether unworthy of the greatness this opportunity had thrust upon him. What was interesting was that he would boast of it openly.

He used to say: 'People think I make a lot of money in this schooner of mine. But that is nothing. I don't care for that. Now and then I go away quietly and lift a bar of silver. I must get rich slowly—you understand.'

There was also another curious point about the man. Once in the course of some quarrel the sailor threatened him: 'What's to prevent me reporting ashore what you have told me about that silver?'

The cynical ruffian was not alarmed in the least. He actually laughed. 'You fool, if you dare talk like that

on shore about me you will get a knife stuck in your
back. Every man, woman, and child in that port is my
friend. And who 's to prove the lighter wasn't sunk?
I didn't show you where the silver is hidden. Did I?
So you know nothing. And suppose I lied? Eh ?'

Ultimately the sailor, disgusted with the sordid mean-
ness of that impenitent thief, deserted from the schooner.
The whole episode takes about three pages of his autobiography. Nothing to speak of; but as I looked them
over, the curious confirmation of the few casual words
heard in my early youth evoked the memories of that
distant time when everything was so fresh, so surprising,
so venturesome, so interesting; bits of strange coasts under
the stars, shadows of hills in the sunshine, men's passions
in the dusk, gossip half forgotten, faces grown dim. . . .
Perhaps, perhaps, there still was in the world something
to write about. Yet I did not see anything at first in the
mere story. A rascal steals a large parcel of a valuable
commodity—so people say. It 's either true or untrue;
and in any case it has no value in itself. To invent a cir-
cumstantial account of the robbery did not appeal to me,
because my talents not running that way I did not think
that the game was worth the candle. It was only when
it dawned upon me that the purloiner of the treasure need
not necessarily be a confirmed rogue, that he could be
even a man of character, an actor and possibly a victim
in the changing scenes of a revolution, it was only then
that I had the first vision of a twilight country which was
to become the province of Sulaco, with its high shadowy
Sierra and its misty Campo for mute witnesses of events
flowing from the passions of men short-sighted in good
and evil.

G

Such are in very truth the obscure origins of *Nostromo*
—the book.   From that moment, I suppose, it had to be.
Yet even then I hesitated, as if warned by the instinct of
self-preservation from venturing on a distant and toilsome
journey into a land full of intrigues and revolutions.   But
it had to be done.

It took the best part of the years 1903–4 to do; with
many intervals of renewed hesitation, lest I should lose
myself in the ever-enlarging vistas opening before me as
I progressed deeper in my knowledge of the country.
Often, also, when I had thought myself to a standstill
over the tangled-up affairs of the Republic, I would,
figuratively speaking, pack my bag, rush away from Sulaco
for a change of air, and write a few pages of *The Mirror of
the Sea*.   But generally, as I 've said before, my sojourn
on the continent of Latin America, famed for its hospi-
tality, lasted for about two years.   On my return I found
(speaking somewhat in the style of Captain Gulliver) my
family all well, my wife heartily glad to learn that the
fuss was all over, and our small boy considerably grown
during my absence.

My principal authority for the history of Costaguana is,
of course, my venerated friend, the late Don José Avellanos, Minister to the Courts of England and Spain, etc.
etc., in his impartial and eloquent *History of Fifty Years
of Misrule*.   That work was never published—the reader
will discover why—and I am in fact the only person in
the world possessed of its contents.   I have mastered
them in not a few hours of earnest meditation, and I hope
that my accuracy will be trusted.   In justice to myself,
and to allay the fears of prospective readers, I beg to point
out that the few historical allusions are never dragged in

for the sake of parading my unique erudition, but that each of them is closely related to actuality; either throwing a light on the nature of current events or affecting directly the fortunes of the people of whom I speak.

As to their own histories I have tried to set them down, Aristocracy and People, men and women, Latin and Anglo-Saxon, bandit and politician, with as cool a hand as was possible in the heat and clash of my own conflicting emotions. And after all this is also the story of their conflicts. It is for the reader to say how far they are deserving of interest in their actions and in the secret purposes of their hearts revealed in the bitter necessities of the time. I confess that, for me, that time is the time of firm friendships and unforgotten hospitalities. And in my gratitude I must mention here Mrs. Gould, 'the first lady of Sulaco,' whom we may safely leave to the secret devotion of Dr. Monygham, and Charles Gould, the Idealist-creator of Material Interests, whom we must leave to his mine—from which there is no escape in this world.

About Nostromo, the second of the two racially and socially contrasted men, both captured by the silver of the San Tomé Mine, I feel bound to say something more.

I did not hesitate to make that central figure an Italian. First of all the thing is perfectly credible: Italians were swarming into the Occidental Province at the time, as anybody who will read further can see; and secondly, there was no one who could stand so well by the side of Giorgio Viola the Garibaldino, the Idealist of the old, humanitarian revolutions. For myself I needed there a man of the People as free as possible from his class-conventions and all settled modes of thinking. This is not

a side snarl at conventions. My reasons were not moral
but artistic. Had he been an Anglo-Saxon he would have
tried to get into local politics. But Nostromo does not
aspire to be a leader in a personal game. He does not want
to raise himself above the mass. He is content to feel
himself a power—within the People.

But mainly Nostromo is what he is because I received
the inspiration for him in my early days from a Mediterranean sailor. Those who have read certain pages of
mine will see at once what I mean when I say that Dominic,
the *padrone* of the *Tremolino*, might under given circumstances have been a Nostromo. At any rate Dominic
would have understood the younger man perfectly—if
scornfully. He and I were engaged together in a rather
absurd adventure, but the absurdity does not matter. It
is a real satisfaction to think that in my very young days
there must, after all, have been something in me worthy
to command that man's half-bitter fidelity, his half-ironic
devotion. Many of Nostromo's speeches I have heard first
in Dominic's voice. His hand on the tiller and his
fearless eyes roaming the horizon from within the monkish
hood shadowing his face, he would utter the usual exor-
dium of his remorseless wisdom: 'Vous autres gentils-
hommes!' in a caustic tone that hangs on my ear yet.
Like Nostromo! 'You *hombres finos!*' Very much like
Nostromo. But Dominic the Corsican nursed a certain
pride of ancestry from which my Nostromo is free; for
Nostromo's lineage had to be more ancient still. He is
a man with the weight of countless generations behind
him and no parentage to boast of. . . . Like the People.

In his firm grip on the earth he inherits, in his im-
providence and generosity, in his lavishness with his gifts,

in his manly vanity, in the obscure sense of his greatness,
and in his faithful devotion with something despairing as
well as desperate in its impulses, he is a Man of the
People, their very own unenvious force, disdaining to
lead but ruling from within.   Years afterwards, grown
older as the famous Captain Fidanza, with a stake in the
country, going about his many affairs followed by respect-
ful glances in the modernized streets of Sulaco, calling on
the widow of the *cargador*, attending the Lodge, listening
in unmoved silence to anarchist speeches at the meeting,
the enigmatical patron of the new revolutionary agitation,
the trusted, the wealthy comrade Fidanza with the knowledge of his moral ruin locked up in his breast, he remains
essentially a Man of the People.   In his mingled love and
scorn of life and in the bewildered conviction of having
been betrayed, of dying betrayed he hardly knows by what
or by whom, he is still of the People, their undoubted
Great Man—with a private history of his own.

One more figure of those stirring times I would like to
mention: and that is Antonia Avellanos—the 'beautiful
Antonia.'   Whether she is a possible variation of Latin-
American girlhood I wouldn't dare to affirm.   But, for
me, she *is*.   Always a little in the background by the side
of her father (my venerated friend) I hope she has yet
relief enough to make intelligible what I am going to say.
Of all the people who had seen with me the birth of the
Occidental Republic, she is the only one who has kept
in my memory the aspect of continued life.   Antonia the
Aristocrat and Nostromo the Man of the People are the
artisans of the New Era, the true creators of the New
State; he by his legendary and daring feat, she, like a
woman, simply by the force of what she is: the only being

capable of inspiring a sincere passion in the heart of a trifler.

If anything could induce me to revisit Sulaco (I should hate to see all these changes) it would be Antonia. And the true reason for that—why not be frank about it?—the true reason is that I have modelled her on my first love. How we, a band of tallish schoolboys, the chums of her two brothers, how we used to look up to that girl just out of the schoolroom herself, as the standard-bearer of a faith to which we all were born but which she alone knew how to hold aloft with an unflinching hope! She had perhaps more glow and less serenity in her soul than Antonia, but she was an uncompromising Puritan of patriotism with no taint of the slightest worldliness in her thoughts. I was not the only one in love with her; but it was I who had to hear oftenest her scathing criticism of my levities—very much like poor Decoud—or stand the brunt of her austere, unanswerable invective. She did not quite understand—but never mind. That afternoon when I came in, a shrinking yet defiant sinner, to say the final good-bye I received a hand-squeeze that made my heart leap and saw a tear that took my breath away. She was softened at the last as though she had suddenly perceived (we were such children still!) that I was really going away for good, going very far away—even as far as Sulaco, lying unknown, hidden from our eyes in the darkness of the Placid Gulf.

That's why I long sometimes for another glimpse of the 'beautiful Antonia' (or can it be the Other?) moving in the dimness of the great cathedral, saying a short prayer at the tomb of the first and last Cardinal-Archbishop of Sulaco, standing absorbed in filial devotion before the monument of Don José Avellanos, and, with a lingering, tender, faithful glance at the medallion-memorial to Martin Decoud, going out serenely into the sunshine of the Plaza with her upright carriage and her white head; a relic of the past disregarded by men awaiting impatiently the Dawns of other New Eras, the coming of more Revolutions.

But this is the idlest of dreams; for I did understand perfectly well at the time that the moment the breath left the body of the Magnificent Capataz, the Man of the People, freed at last from the toils of love and wealth, there was nothing more for me to do in Sulaco.

*October 1917.* J. C.

# THE MIRROR OF THE SEA

Memories and Impressions

*Published in* 1906

# THE MIRROR OF THE SEA

Less perhaps than any other book written by me, or anybody else, does this volume require a preface. Yet since all the others, including even the *Personal Record*, which is but a fragment of biography, are to have their Author's Notes I cannot possibly leave this one without, lest a false impression of indifference or weariness should be created. I can see only too well that it is not going to be an easy task. Necessity—the mother of invention —being even unthinkable in this case, I do not know what to invent in the way of discourse; and necessity being also the greatest possible incentive to exertion I don't even know how to begin to exert myself. Here, too, the natural inclination comes in. I have been all my life averse from exertion.

Under these discouraging circumstances I am, however, bound to proceed from a sense of duty. This Note is a thing promised. In less than a minute's time, by a few incautious words I entered into a bond which has lain on my heart heavily ever since.

For, this book is a very intimate revelation; and what that is revealing can a few more pages add to some three hundred others of most sincere disclosures? I have attempted here to lay bare with the unreserve of a last hour's confession the terms of my relation with the sea, which beginning mysteriously, like any great passion the inscrutable Gods send to mortals, went on unreasoning and invincible, surviving the test of disillusion, defying the disenchantment that lurks in every day of a strenuous life; went on full of love's delight and love's anguish, facing them in open-eyed exultation, without bitterness and without repining, from the first hour to the last.

Subjugated but never unmanned I surrendered my being to that passion which, various and great like life itself, had also its periods of wonderful serenity which even a fickle mistress can give sometimes on her soothed breast, full of wiles, full of fury, and yet capable of an enchanting sweetness. And if anybody suggests that this must be the lyric illusion of an old, romantic heart, I can answer that for twenty years I had lived like a hermit with my passion! Beyond the line of the sea horizon the world for me did not exist as assuredly as it does not exist for the mystics who take refuge on the tops of high mountains. I am speaking now of that innermost life, containing the best and the worst that can happen to us in the temperamental depths of our being, where a man indeed must live alone but need not give up all hope of holding converse with his kind.

This perhaps is enough for me to say on this particular occasion about these, my parting words, about this, my last mood in my great passion for the sea. I call it great because it was great to me. Others may call it a foolish infatuation. Those words have been applied to every love story. But whatever it may be the fact remains that it was something too great for words.

This is what I always felt vaguely; and therefore the following pages rest like a true confession on matters of fact which to a friendly and charitable person may convey the inner truth of almost a lifetime. From sixteen to thirty-six cannot be called an age, yet it is a pretty long stretch of that sort of experience which teaches a man slowly to see and feel. It is for me a distinct period; and when I emerged from it into another air, as it were, and said to myself: 'Now I must speak of these things or remain unknown to the end of my days,' it was with the ineradicable hope, that accompanies one through solitude as well as through a crowd, of ultimately, some day, at some moment, making myself understood.

And I have been! I have been understood as completely as it is possible to be understood in this, our world, which seems to be mostly composed of riddles. There have been things said about this book which have moved me profoundly; the more profoundly because they were uttered by men whose occupation was avowedly to understand, and analyse, and expound—in a word, by literary critics. They spoke out according to their conscience, and some of them said things that made me feel both glad and sorry of ever having entered upon my confession. Dimly or clearly, they perceived the character of my intention and ended by judging me worthy to have made the attempt. They saw it was of a revealing character, but in some cases they thought that the revelation was not complete.

One of them said: 'In reading these chapters one is always hoping for the revelation; but the personality is never quite revealed. We can only say that this thing happened to Mr. Conrad, that he knew such a man and that thus life passed him leaving those memories. They are the records of the events of his life, not in every instance striking or decisive events but rather those haphazard events which for no definite reason impress themselves upon the mind and recur in memory long afterward as symbols of one knows not what sacred ritual taking place behind the veil.'

To this I can only say that this book written in perfect sincerity holds back nothing—unless the mere bodily presence of the writer. Within these pages I make a full confession not of my sins but of my emotions. It is the best tribute my piety can offer to the ultimate shapers of my character, convictions, and, in a sense, destiny—to the imperishable sea, to the ships that are no more, and to the simple men who have had their day.

1919.                                                   J. C.

# THE SECRET AGENT

A Simple Tale

*Published in* 1907

# THE SECRET AGENT

The origin of *The Secret Agent*: subject, treatment, artistic purpose, and every other motive that may induce an author to take up his pen, can, I believe, be traced to a period of mental and emotional reaction.

The actual facts are that I began this book impulsively and wrote it continuously. When in due course it was bound and delivered to the public gaze I found myself reproved for having produced it at all. Some of the admonitions were severe, others had a sorrowful note. I have not got them textually before me but I remember perfectly the general argument, which was very simple; and also my surprise at its nature. All this sounds a very old story now! And yet it is not such a long time ago. I must conclude that I had still preserved much of my pristine innocence in the year 1907. It seems to me now that even an artless person might have foreseen that some criticisms would be based on the ground of sordid surroundings and the moral squalor of the tale.

That of course is a serious objection. It was not universal. In fact it seems ungracious to remember so little reproof amongst so much intelligent and sympathetic appreciation; and I trust that the readers of this Preface will not hasten to put it down to wounded vanity or a natural disposition to ingratitude. I suggest that a charitable heart could very well ascribe my choice to natural modesty. Yet it isn't exactly modesty that makes me select reproof for the illustration of my case. No, it

H

isn't exactly modesty.   I am not at all certain that I am
modest; but those who have read so far through my work
will credit me with enough decency, tact, *savoir-faire*,
what you will, to prevent me from making a song for my
own glory out of the words of other people.   No!   The
true motive of my selection lies in quite a different trait.
I have always had a propensity to justify my action.   Not
to defend.   To justify.   Not to insist that I was right but
simply to explain that there was no perverse intention,
no secret scorn for the natural sensibilities of mankind at
the bottom of my impulses.

That kind of weakness is dangerous only so far that it
exposes one to the risk of becoming a bore; for the world
generally is not interested in the motives of any overt act
but in its consequences.   Man may smile and smile but
he is not an investigating animal.   He loves the obvious.
He shrinks from explanations.   Yet I will go on with
mine.   It's obvious that I need not have written that
book.   I was under no necessity to deal with that subject;
using the word subject both in the sense of the tale itself
and in the larger one of a special manifestation in the life
of mankind.   This I fully admit.   But the thought of
elaborating mere ugliness in order to shock, or even
simply to surprise my readers by a change of front, has
never entered my head.   In making this statement I expect
to be believed, not only on the evidence of my general
character but also for the reason, which anybody can
see, that the whole treatment of the tale, its inspiring
indignation and underlying pity and contempt, prove my
detachment from the squalor and sordidness which lie
simply in the outward circumstances of the setting.

The inception of *The Secret Agent* followed immediately

on a two years' period of intense absorption in the task
of writing that remote novel, *Nostromo*, with its far-off
Latin-American atmosphere; and the profoundly personal
*Mirror of the Sea*.   The first an intense creative effort on
what I suppose will always remain my largest canvas, the
second an unreserved attempt to unveil for a moment
the profounder intimacies of the sea and the formative
influences of nearly half my lifetime.   It was a period,
too, in which my sense of the truth of things was attended
by a very intense imaginative and emotional readiness
which, all genuine and faithful to facts as it was, yet
made me feel (the task once done) as if I were left behind,
aimless amongst mere husks of sensations and lost in a
world of other, of inferior, values.

I don't know whether I really felt that I wanted a
change, change in my imagination, in my vision, and in
my mental attitude.   I rather think that a change in the
fundamental mood had already stolen over me unawares.
I don't remember anything definite happening.   With
*The Mirror of the Sea* finished in the full consciousness that
I had dealt honestly with myself and my readers in every
line of that book, I gave myself up to a not unhappy pause.
Then, while I was yet standing still, as it were, and certainly not thinking of going out of my way to look for
anything ugly, the subject of *The Secret Agent*—I mean the
tale—came to me in the shape of a few words uttered
by a friend in a casual conversation about anarchists or
rather anarchist activities; how brought about I don't
remember now.

I remember, however, remarking on the criminal futility
of the whole thing, doctrine, action, mentality; and on
the contemptible aspect of the half-crazy pose as of a

brazen cheat exploiting the poignant miseries and passionate credulities of a mankind always so tragically eager
for self-destruction. That was what made for me its
philosophical pretences so unpardonable. Presently, passing to particular instances, we recalled the already old
story of the attempt to blow up the Greenwich Observatory; a blood-stained inanity of so fatuous a kind that it
was impossible to fathom its origin by any reasonable or
even unreasonable process of thought. For perverse un-
reason has its own logical processes. But that outrage
could not be laid hold of mentally in any sort of way, so
that one remained faced by the fact of a man blown to
bits for nothing even most remotely resembling an idea,
anarchistic or other. As to the outer wall of the Observatory it did not show as much as the faintest crack.

I pointed all this out to my friend, who remained silent
for a while and then remarked in his characteristically
casual and omniscient manner: 'Oh, that fellow was half
an idiot. His sister committed suicide afterwards.' These
were absolutely the only words that passed between us;
for extreme surprise at this unexpected piece of information kept me dumb for a moment and he began at once
to talk of something else. It never occurred to me later
to ask how he arrived at his knowledge. I am sure that
if he had seen once in his life the back of an anarchist
that must have been the whole extent of his connection
with the underworld. He was, however, a man who
liked to talk with all sorts of people, and he may have
gathered those illuminating facts at second or third hand,
from a crossing-sweeper, from a retired police officer,
from some vague man in his club, or even, perhaps, from a
Minister of State met at some public or private reception.

Of the illuminating quality there could be no doubt whatever. One felt like walking out of a forest on to a plain—there was not much to see but one had plenty of light. No, there was not much to see and, frankly, for a considerable time I didn't even attempt to perceive anything. It was only the illuminating impression that remained. It remained satisfactory but in a passive way. Then, about a week later, I came upon a book which as far as I know had never attained any prominence, the rather summary recollections of an Assistant Commissioner of Police, an obviously able man with a strong religious strain in his character who was appointed to his post at the time of the dynamite outrages in London, away back in the eighties. The book was fairly interesting, very discreet of course; and I have by now forgotten the bulk of its contents. It contained no revelations, it ran over the surface agreeably, and that was all. I won't even try to explain why I should have been arrested by a little passage of about seven lines, in which the author (I believe his name was Anderson) reproduced a short dialogue held in the lobby of the House of Commons after some un-expected anarchist outrage, with the Home Secretary. I think it was Sir William Harcourt then. He was very much irritated and the official was very apologetic. The phrase, amongst the three which passed between them, that struck me most was Sir W. Harcourt's angry sally: 'All that's very well. But your idea of secrecy over there seems to consist of keeping the Home Secretary in the dark.' Characteristic enough of Sir W. Harcourt's temper but not much in itself. There must have been, however, some sort of atmosphere in the whole incident because all of a sudden I felt myself stimulated. And

then ensued in my mind what a student of chemistry
would best understand from the analogy of the addition
of the tiniest little drop of the right kind, precipitating
the process of crystallization in a test-tube containing
some colourless solution.

It was at first for me a mental change, disturbing a
quieted-down imagination, in which strange forms, sharp
in outline but imperfectly apprehended, appeared and
claimed attention as crystals will do by their bizarre and
unexpected shapes.   One fell to musing before the phenomenon—even of the past: of South America, a continent
of crude sunshine and brutal revolutions, of the sea, the
vast expanse of salt waters, the mirror of heaven's frowns
and smiles, the reflector of the world's light.   Then the
vision of an enormous town presented itself, of a monstrous town more populous than some continents and in
its man-made might as if indifferent to heaven's frowns
and smiles; a cruel devourer of the world's light.   There
was room enough there to place any story, depth enough
there for any passion, variety enough there for any setting,
darkness enough to bury five millions of lives.

Irresistibly the town became the background for the
ensuing period of deep and tentative meditations.   End-
less vistas opened before me in various directions.   It
would take years to find the right way!   It seemed to
take years! . . . Slowly the dawning conviction of Mrs.
Verloc's maternal passion grew up to a flame between me
and that background, tingeing it with its secret ardour
and receiving from it in exchange some of its own sombre
colouring.   At last the story of Winnie Verloc stood out
complete from the days of her childhood to the end, un-
proportioned as yet, with everything still on the first

plan, as it were; but ready now to be dealt with.  It was a matter of about three days.

*This* book is *that* story, reduced to manageable proportions, its whole course suggested and centred round the absurd cruelty of the Greenwich Park explosion.  I had there a task I will not say arduous but of the most absorbing difficulty.  But it had to be done.  It was a necessity. The figures grouped about Mrs. Verloc and related directly or indirectly to her tragic suspicion that 'life doesn't stand much looking into,' are the outcome of that very necessity. Personally I have never had any doubt of the reality of Mrs. Verloc's story; but it had to be disengaged from its obscurity in that immense town, it had to be made credible, I don't mean so much as to her soul but as to her surroundings, not so much as to her psychology but as to her humanity.   For the surroundings hints were not lacking.   I had to fight hard to keep at arm's length the memories of my solitary and nocturnal walks all over London in my early days, lest they should rush in and overwhelm each page of the story as these emerged one after another from a mood as serious in feeling and thought as any in which I ever wrote a line.   In that respect I really think that *The Secret Agent* is a perfectly genuine piece of work.   Even the purely artistic purpose, that of applying an ironic method to a subject of that kind, was formulated with deliberation and in the earnest belief that ironic treatment alone would enable me to say all I felt I would have to say in scorn as well as in pity.   It is one of the minor satisfactions of my writing life that having taken that resolve I did manage, it seems to me, to carry it right through to the end.   As to the personages whom the absolute necessity of the case—Mrs. Verloc's case—brings out in front of the London background, from them, too, I obtained those little satisfactions which really count for so much against the mass of oppressive doubts that haunt so persistently every attempt at creative work. For instance, of Mr. Vladimir himself (who was fair game for a caricatural presentation) I was gratified to hear that an experienced man of the world had said 'that Conrad must have been in touch with that sphere or else has an excellent intuition of things,' because Mr. Vladimir was 'not only possible in detail but quite right in essentials.' Then a visitor from America informed me that all sorts of revolutionary refugees in New York would have it that the book was written by somebody who knew a lot about them. This seemed to me a very high compliment, considering that, as a matter of hard fact, I had seen even less of their kind than the omniscient friend who gave me the first suggestion for the novel. I have no doubt, however, that there had been moments during the writing of the book when I was an extreme revolutionist, I won't say more convinced than they but certainly cherishing a more concentrated purpose than any of them had ever done in the whole course of his life. I don't say this to boast. I was simply attending to my business. In the matter of all my books I have always attended to my business. I have attended to it with complete self-surrender. And this statement, too, is not a boast. I could not have done otherwise. It would have bored me too much to make believe.

The suggestions for certain personages of the tale, both law-abiding and lawless, came from various sources which, perhaps, here and there, some reader may have recognized. They are not very recondite. But I am not concerned here to legitimize any of those people, and even as to my general view of the moral reactions as between the criminal and the police all I will venture to say is that it seems to me to be at least arguable.

The twelve years that have elapsed since the publication of the book have not changed my attitude. I do not regret having written it. Lately, circumstances, which have nothing to do with the general tenor of this preface, have compelled me to strip this tale of the literary robe of indignant scorn it had cost me so much to fit on it decently, years ago. I have been forced, so to speak, to look upon its bare bones. I confess that it makes a grisly skeleton. But still I will submit that telling Winnie Verloc's story to its anarchistic end of utter desolation, madness, and despair, and telling it as I have told it here, I have not intended to commit a gratuitous outrage on the feelings of mankind.

1920.                                          J. C.

# A SET OF SIX

A Romantic Tale : Gaspar Ruiz
An Ironic Tale : The Informer
An Indignant Tale : The Brute
A Desperate Tale : An Anarchist
A Military Tale : The Duel
A Pathetic Tale : Il Conde

*Published in* 1908

# A SET OF SIX

The six stories in this volume are the result of some three or four years of occasional work. The dates of their writing are far apart, their origins are various. None of them are connected directly with personal experiences. In all of them the facts are inherently true, by which I mean that they are not only possible but that they have actually happened. For instance, the last story in the volume, the one I call *Pathetic*, whose first title is *Il Conde* (mis-spelt by the by), is an almost verbatim transcript of the tale told me by a very charming old gentleman whom I met in Italy. I don't mean to say it is only that. Anybody can see that it is something more than a verbatim report, but where he left off and where I began must be left to the acute discrimination of the reader who may be interested in the problem. I don't mean to say that the problem is worth the trouble. What I am certain of, however, is that it is not to be solved, for I am not at all clear about it myself by this time. All I can say is that the personality of the narrator was extremely suggestive quite apart from the story he was telling me. I heard a few years ago that he had died far away from his beloved Naples where that 'abominable adventure' did really happen to him.

Thus the genealogy of *Il Conde* is simple. It is not the case with the other stories. Various strains contributed to their composition, and the nature of many of those I have forgotten, not having the habit of making notes either before or after the fact.   I mean the fact of writing a story.   What I remember best about *Gaspar Ruiz* is that it was written, or at any rate begun, within a month of finishing *Nostromo*; but apart from the locality, and that a pretty wide one (all the South American continent), the novel and the story have nothing in common, neither mood nor intention, and, certainly, not the style.   The manner for the most part is that of General Santierra, and that old warrior, I note with satisfaction, is very true to himself all through.   Looking now dispassionately at the various ways in which this story could have been presented I can't honestly think the General superfluous.   It is he, an old man talking of the days of his youth, who characterizes the whole narrative and gives it an air of actuality which I doubt whether I could have achieved without his help.   In the mere writing his existence of course was of no help at all, because the whole thing had to be carefully kept within the frame of his simple mind.   But all this is but a laborious searching of memories.   My present feeling is that the story could not have been told otherwise.   The hint for Gaspar Ruiz the man I found in a book by Captain Basil Hall, R.N., who was for some time, between the years 1824 and 1828, senior officer of a small British squadron on the west coast of South America.   His book, published in the thirties, obtained a certain celebrity and I suppose is to be found still in some libraries.   The curious who may be mistrusting my imagination are referred to that printed document, volume two, I forget the page, but it is somewhere not far from the end.   Another document connected with this story is a letter of a biting and ironic kind from a friend then in Burma, passing certain strictures upon 'the gentleman with the gun on his back' which I do not intend to make accessible to the public. Yet the gun episode did really happen, or at least I am bound to believe it because I remember it, described in an extremely matter-of-fact tone, in some book I read in my boyhood; and I am not going to discard the beliefs of my boyhood for anybody on earth.

*The Brute*, which is the only sea-story in the volume, is, like *Il Conde*, associated with a direct narrative and based on a suggestion gathered on warm human lips. I will not disclose the real name of the criminal ship but the first I heard of her homicidal habits was from the late Captain Blake, commanding a London ship in which I served in 1884 as second officer. Captain Blake was, of all my commanders, the one I remember with the greatest affection. I have sketched in his personality, without, however, mentioning his name, in the first paper of *The Mirror of the Sea*. In his young days he had had a personal experience of the brute, and it is perhaps for that reason that I have put the story into the mouth of a young man and made of it what the reader will see. The existence of the brute was a fact. The end of the brute as related in the story is also a fact, well known at the time though it really happened to another ship, of great beauty of form and of blameless character, which certainly deserved a better fate. I have unscrupulously adapted it to the needs of my story, thinking that I had there something in the nature of poetical justice. I hope that little villainy will not cast a shadow upon the general honesty of my proceedings as a writer of tales.

Of *The Informer* and *The Anarchist* I will say next to nothing. The pedigree of these tales is hopelessly

complicated and not worth disentangling at this distance
of time.  I found them and here they are.  The discrimin-
ating reader will guess that I have found them within my
mind; but how they or their elements came in there I
have forgotten for the most part; and for the rest I really
don't see why I should give myself away more than I have
done already.

It remains for me only now to mention *The Duel*, the
longest story in the book.  That story attained the dignity
of publication all by itself in a small illustrated volume,
under the title, *The Point of Honour*.  That was many
years ago.  It has been since reinstated in its proper place,
which is the place it occupies in this volume, in all the
subsequent editions of my work.  Its pedigree is extremely
simple.  It springs from a ten-line paragraph in a small
provincial paper published in the south of France.  That
paragraph, occasioned by a duel with a fatal ending between
two well-known Parisian personalities, referred for some
reason or other to the 'well-known fact' of two officers
in Napoleon's Grand Army having fought a series of duels
in the midst of great wars and on some futile pretext.
The pretext was never disclosed.  I had therefore to
invent it; and I think that, given the character of the
two officers, which I had to invent, too, I have made it
sufficiently convincing by the mere force of its absurdity.
The truth is that in my mind the story is nothing but a
serious and even earnest attempt at a bit of historical
fiction.  I had heard in my boyhood a good deal of the
great Napoleonic legend.  I had a genuine feeling that
I would find myself at home in it, and *The Duel* is the
result of that feeling, or, if the reader prefers, of that
presumption.  Personally I have no qualms of conscience

about this piece of work. The story might have been better told, of course. All one's work might have been better done; but this is the sort of reflection a worker must put aside courageously if he doesn't mean every one of his conceptions to remain for ever a private vision, an evanescent reverie. How many of those visions have I seen vanish in my time! This one, however, has remained, a testimony, if you like, to my courage or a proof of my rashness. What I care to remember best is the testimony of some French readers who volunteered the opinion that in those hundred pages or so I had managed to render 'wonderfully' the spirit of the whole epoch. Exaggeration of kindness no doubt; but even so I hug it still to my breast, because in truth that is exactly what I was trying to capture in my small net: the Spirit of the Epoch—never purely militarist in the long clash of arms, youthful, almost childlike in its exaltation of sentiment—naïvely heroic in its faith.

1920.                                    J. C.

# UNDER WESTERN EYES

*Published in* 1911

# UNDER WESTERN EYES

It must be admitted that by the mere force of circumstances *Under Western Eyes* has become already a sort of historical novel dealing with the past.

This reflection bears entirely upon the events of the tale; but being as a whole an attempt to render not so much the political state as the psychology of Russia itself, I venture to hope that it has not lost all its interest. I am encouraged in this flattering belief by noticing that in many articles on Russian affairs of the present day reference is made to certain sayings and opinions uttered in the pages that follow, in a manner testifying to the clearness of my vision and the correctness of my judgment. I need not say that in writing this novel I had no other object in view than to express imaginatively the general truth which underlies its action, together with my honest convictions as to the moral complexion of certain facts more or less known to the whole world.

As to the actual creation I may say that when I began to write I had a distinct conception of the first part only, with the three figures of Haldin, Razumov, and Councillor Mikulin, defined exactly in my mind. It was only after I had finished writing the first part that the whole story revealed itself to me in its tragic character and in the march of its events as unavoidable and sufficiently ample in its outline to give free play to my creative instinct and to the dramatic possibilities of the subject.

The course of action need not be explained. It has

suggested itself more as a matter of feeling than a matter of thinking. It is the result not of a special experience but of general knowledge, fortified by earnest meditation. My greatest anxiety was in being able to strike and sustain the note of scrupulous impartiality. The obligation of absolute fairness was imposed on me historically and hereditarily, by the peculiar experience of race and family, in addition to my primary conviction that truth alone is the justification of any fiction which makes the least claim to the quality of art or may hope to take its place in the culture of men and women of its time. I had never been called before to a greater effort of detachment: detachment from all passions, prejudices, and even from personal memories. *Under Western Eyes* on its first appearance in England was a failure with the public, perhaps because of that very detachment. I obtained my reward some six years later when I first heard that the book had found universal recognition in Russia and had been republished there in many editions.

The various figures playing their part in the story also owe their existence to no special experience but to the general knowledge of the condition of Russia and of the moral and emotional reactions of the Russian temperament to the pressure of tyrannical lawlessness, which, in general human terms, could be reduced to the formula of senseless desperation provoked by senseless tyranny. What I was concerned with mainly was the aspect, the character, and the fate of the individuals as they appeared to the Western Eyes of the old teacher of languages. He himself has been much criticized; but I will not at this late hour undertake to justify his existence. He was useful to me and therefore I think that he must be useful to the reader both in the way of comment and by the part he plays in the development of the story. In my desire to produce the effect of actuality it seemed to me indispensable to have an eye-witness of the transactions in Geneva. I needed also a sympathetic friend for Miss Haldin, who otherwise would have been too much alone and unsupported to be perfectly credible. She would have had no one to whom she could give a glimpse of her idealistic faith, of her great heart, and of her simple emotions.

Razumov is treated sympathetically. Why should he not be? He is an ordinary young man, with a healthy capacity for work and sane ambitions. He has an average conscience. If he is slightly abnormal it is only in his sensitiveness to his position. Being nobody's child he feels rather more keenly than another would that he is a Russian—or he is nothing. He is perfectly right in looking on all Russia as his heritage. The sanguinary futility of the crimes and the sacrifices seething in that amorphous mass envelops and crushes him. But I don't think that in his distraction he is ever monstrous. No-body is exhibited as a monster here—neither the simple-minded Tekla nor the wrong-headed Sophia Antonovna. Peter Ivanovitch and Madame de S. are fair game. They are the apes of a sinister jungle and are treated as their grimaces deserve. As to Nikita—nicknamed Necator—he is the perfect flower of the terroristic wilderness. What troubled me most in dealing with him was not his monstrosity but his banality. He has been exhibited to the public eye for years in so-called 'disclosures' in news-paper articles, in secret histories, in sensational novels.

The most terrifying reflection (I am speaking now for

myself) is that all these people are not the product of the exceptional but of the general—of the normality of their place, and time, and race.  The ferocity and imbecility of an autocratic rule rejecting all legality and in fact basing itself upon complete moral anarchism provokes the no less imbecile and atrocious answer of a purely Utopian revolutionism encompassing destruction by the first means to hand, in the strange conviction that a fundamental change of hearts must follow the downfall of any given human institutions.   These people are unable to see that all they can effect is merely a change of names. The oppressors and the oppressed are all Russians together; and the world is brought once more face to face with the truth of the saying that the tiger cannot change his stripes nor the leopard his spots.

1920.                                                     J. C.

# A PERSONAL RECORD

*Originally published as*

# SOME REMINISCENCES

*in* 1912

# A PERSONAL RECORD

The reissue of this book in a new form does not, strictly speaking, require another Preface.[1] But since this is distinctly a place for personal remarks I take the opportunity to refer in this Author's Note to two points arising from certain statements about myself I have noticed of late in the press.

One of them bears upon the question of language. I have always felt myself looked upon somewhat in the light of a phenomenon, a position which outside the circus world cannot be regarded as desirable. It needs a special temperament for one to derive much gratification from the fact of being able to do freakish things intentionally, and, as it were, from mere vanity.

The fact of my not writing in my native language has been of course commented upon frequently in reviews and notices of my various works and in the more extended critical articles. I suppose that was unavoidable; and indeed these comments were of the most flattering kind to one's vanity. But in that matter I have no vanity that could be flattered. I could not have it. The first object of this note is to disclaim any merit there might have been in an act of deliberate volition.

The impression of my having exercised a choice between the two languages, French and English, both foreign to me, has got abroad somehow. That impression is erroneous. It originated, I believe, in an article written by Sir Hugh

1 See Appendix page 199.

Clifford and published in the year '98, I think, of the last century.   Some time before, Sir Hugh Clifford came to see me.   He is, if not the first, then one of the first two friends I made for myself by my work, the other being Mr. Cunninghame Graham, who, characteristically enough, had been captivated by my story, *An Outpost of Progress*. These friendships which have endured to this day I count amongst my precious possessions.

Mr. Hugh Clifford (he was not decorated then) had just published his first volume of Malay sketches.   I was naturally delighted to see him and infinitely gratified by the kind things he found to say about my first books and some of my early short stories, the action of which is placed in the Malay Archipelago.   I remember that after saying many things which ought to have made me blush to the roots of my hair with outraged modesty, he ended by telling me with the uncompromising yet kindly firmness of a man accustomed to speak unpalatable truths even to Oriental potentates (for their own good of course) that as a matter of fact I didn't know anything about Malays.   I was perfectly aware of this.   I have never pretended to any such knowledge, and I was moved—I wonder to this day at my impertinence—to retort: 'Of course I don't know anything about Malays.   If I knew only one hundredth part of what you and Frank Swettenham know of Malays I would make everybody sit up.'   He went on looking kindly (but firmly) at me and then we both burst out laughing.   In the course of that most welcome visit twenty years ago, which I remember so well, we talked of many things; the characteristics of various languages was one of them, and it is on that day that my friend carried away with him the impression that I had exercised a

deliberate choice between French and English. Later,
when moved by his friendship (no empty word to him)
to write a study in the *North American Review* on Joseph
Conrad, he conveyed that impression to the public.

This misapprehension, for it is nothing else, was no
doubt my fault. I must have expressed myself badly in
the course of a friendly and intimate talk when one doesn't
watch one's phrases carefully. My recollection of what
I meant to say is: that *had I been under the necessity* of making
a choice between the two, and though I knew French
fairly well and was familiar with it from infancy, I would
have been afraid to attempt expression in a language so
perfectly 'crystallized.' This, I believe, was the word
I used. And then we passed to other matters. I had to
tell him a little about myself; and what he told me of his
work in the East, his own particular East of which I had
but the mistiest, short glimpse, was of the most absorbing
interest. The present Governor of Nigeria may not
remember that conversation as well as I do, but I am sure
that he will not mind this, what in diplomatic language
is called 'rectification' of a statement made to him by
an obscure writer his generous sympathy had prompted
him to seek out and make his friend.

The truth of the matter is that my faculty to write in
English is as natural as any other aptitude with which I
might have been born. I have a strange and overpowering
feeling that it had always been an inherent part of myself.
English was for me neither a matter of choice nor adoption. The merest idea of choice had never entered my
head. And as to adoption—well, yes, there was adoption; but it was I who was adopted by the genius of the
language, which directly I came out of the stammering

stage made me its own so completely that its very idioms I truly believe had a direct action on my temperament and fashioned my still plastic character.

It was a very intimate action and for that very reason it is too mysterious to explain.   The task would be as impossible as trying to explain love at first sight.   There was something in this conjunction of exulting, almost physical recognition, the same sort of emotional surrender and the same pride of possession, all united in the wonder of a great discovery; but there was on it none of that shadow of dreadful doubt that falls on the very flame of our perishable passions.   One knew very well that this was for ever.

A matter of discovery and not of inheritance, that very inferiority of the title makes the faculty still more precious, lays the possessor under a lifelong obligation to remain worthy of his great fortune.   But it seems to me that all this sounds as if I were trying to explain—a task which I have just pronounced to be impossible.   If in action we may admit with awe that the Impossible recedes before men's indomitable spirit, the Impossible in matters of analysis will always make a stand at some point or other. All I can claim after all those years of devoted practice, with the accumulated anguish of its doubts, imperfections and falterings in my heart, is the right to be believed when I say that if I had not written in English I would not have written at all.

The other remark which I wish to make here is also a rectification but of a less direct kind.   It has nothing to do with the medium of expression.   It bears on the matter of my authorship in another way.   It is not for me to criticize my judges, the more so because I always felt that I was receiving more than justice at their hands. But it seems to me that their unfailingly interested sympathy has ascribed to racial and historical influences much of what, I believe, appertains simply to the individual. Nothing is more foreign than what in the literary world is called Sclavonism, to the Polish temperament with its tradition of self-government, its chivalrous view of moral restraints, and an exaggerated respect for individual rights: not to mention the important fact that the whole Polish mentality, Western in complexion, had received its training from Italy and France and, historically, had always remained, even in religious matters, in sympathy with the most liberal currents of European thought.  An impartial view of humanity in all its degrees of splendour and misery together with a special regard for the rights of the unprivileged of this earth, not on any mystic ground but on the ground of simple fellowship and honourable reciprocity of services, was the dominant characteristic of the mental and moral atmosphere of the houses which sheltered my hazardous childhood: matters of calm and deep conviction both lasting and consistent,  and removed as far as possible from that humanitarianism that seems to be merely a matter of crazy nerves or a morbid conscience.

One of the most sympathetic of my critics tried to account for certain characteristics of my work by the fact of my being, in his own words, 'the son of a Revolutionist.'  No epithet could be more inapplicable to a man with such a strong sense of responsibility in the region of ideas and action and so indifferent to the promptings of personal ambition as my father.  Why the description 'revolutionary' should have been applied all through Europe to the Polish risings of 1831 and 1863 I really cannot understand. These risings were purely revolts against foreign domination. The Russians themselves called them 'rebellions,' which, from their point of view, was the exact truth. Amongst the men concerned in the preliminaries of the 1863 movement my father was no more revolutionary than the others, in the sense of working for the subversion of any social or political scheme of existence. He was simply a patriot in the sense of a man who believing in the spirituality of a national existence could not bear to see that spirit enslaved.

Called out publicly in a kindly attempt to justify the work of the son, that figure of my past cannot be dismissed without a few more words. As a child of course I knew very little of my father's activities, for I was not quite twelve when he died. What I saw with my own eyes was the public funeral, the cleared streets, the hushed crowds; but I understood perfectly well that this was a manifestation of the national spirit seizing a worthy occasion. That bareheaded mass of work people, youths of the University, women at the windows, schoolboys on the pavement, could have known nothing positive about him except the fame of his fidelity to the one guiding emotion in their hearts. I had nothing but that knowledge myself; and this great silent demonstration seemed to me the most natural tribute in the world—not to the man but to the Idea.

What had impressed me much more intimately was the burning of his manuscripts a fortnight or so before his death. It was done under his own superintendence. I happened to go into his room a little earlier than usual that evening, and remaining unnoticed stayed to watch the nursing-sister feeding the blaze in the fire-place.

My father sat in a deep arm-chair propped up with pillows. This is the last time I saw him out of bed. His aspect was to me not so much that of a man desperately ill, as mortally weary—a vanquished man. That act of destruction affected me profoundly by its air of surrender. Not before death, however. To a man of such strong faith death could not have been an enemy.

For many years I believed that every scrap of his writings had been burnt, but in July of 1914 the librarian of the University of Cracow, calling on me during our short visit to Poland, mentioned the existence of a few manuscripts of my father and especially of a series of letters written before and during his exile to his most intimate friend who had sent them to the university for preservation. I went to the library at once, but had only time then for a mere glance. I intended to come back next day and arrange for copies being made of the whole correspondence. But next day there was war. So perhaps I shall never know now what he wrote to his most intimate friend in the time of his domestic happiness, of his new paternity, of his strong hopes—and later, in the hours of disillusion, bereavement and gloom.

I had also imagined him to be completely forgotten forty-five years after his death. But this was not the case. Some young men of letters had discovered him, mostly as a remarkable translator of Shakespeare, Victor Hugo, and Alfred de Vigny, to whose drama *Chatterton*, translated by himself, he had written an eloquent preface defending the poet's deep humanity and his ideal of noble stoicism. The political side of his life was being recalled too; for some men of his time, his co-workers in the task of keeping the national spirit firm in the hope of an inde-

K

pendent future, had been in their old age publishing their
memoirs, where the part he played was for the first time
publicly disclosed to the world.   I learned then of things
in his life I never knew before, things which outside the
group of the initiated could have been known to no living
being except my mother.   It was thus that from a volume
of posthumous ~emoirs dealing with those bitter years
I learned the fact that the first inception of the secret
National Committee intended primarily to organize moral
resistance to the augmented pressure of Russianism arose
on my father's initiative, and that its first meetings were
held in our Warsaw house, of which all I remember
distinctly is one room, white and crimson, probably the
drawing-room.   In one of its walls there was the loftiest
of all archways.   Where it led to remains a mystery; but
to this day I cannot get rid of the belief that all this was
of enormous proportions, and that the people appearing
and disappearing in that immense space were beyond the
usual stature of mankind as I got to know it in later life.
Amongst them I remember my mother, a more familiar
figure than the others, dressed in the black of the national
mourning worn in defiance of ferocious police regulations.
I have also preserved from that particular time the awe
of her mysterious gravity which, indeed, was by no means
smileless.   For I remember her smiles, too.   Perhaps
for me she could always find a smile.   She was young
then, certainly not thirty yet.   She died four years later
in exile.

In the pages which follow I mention her visit to her
brother's house about a year before her death.   I also
speak a little of my father as I remember him in the years
following what was for him the deadly blow of her loss.

And now, having been again evoked in answer to the words of a friendly critic, these Shades may be allowed to return to their place of rest where their forms in life linger yet, dim but poignant, and awaiting the moment when their haunting reality, their last trace on earth, shall pass for ever with me out of the world.

J. C.

1919.

# 'TWIXT LAND AND SEA TALES

A Smile of Fortune
The Secret Sharer
Freya of the Seven Isles

*Published in* 1912

# 'TWIXT LAND AND SEA TALES

The only bond between these three stories is, so to speak, geographical, for their scene, be it land, be it sea, is situated in the same region, which may be called the region of the Indian Ocean with its offshoots and prolongations north of the equator even as far as the Gulf of Siam. In point of time they belong to the period immediately after the publication of that novel with the awkward title *Under Western Eyes* and, as far as the life of the writer is concerned, their appearance in a volume marks a definite change in the fortunes of his fiction. For there is no denying the fact that *Under Western Eyes* found no favour in the public eye, whereas the novel called *Chance* which followed *'Twixt Land and Sea* was received on its first appearance by many more readers than any other of my books.

This volume of three tales was also well received, publicly and privately and from a publisher's point of view. This little success was a most timely tonic for my enfeebled bodily frame. For this may indeed be called the book of a man's convalescence, at least as to three-fourths of it; because *The Secret Sharer*, the middle story, was written much earlier than the other two.

For in truth the memories of *Under Western Eyes* are associated with the memory of a severe illness which seemed to wait like a tiger in the jungle on the turn of a path to jump on me the moment the last words of that

novel were written.  The memory of an illness is very
much like the memory of a nightmare.  On emerging
from it in a much enfeebled state I was inspired to direct
my tottering steps toward the Indian Ocean, a complete
change of surroundings and atmosphere from the Lake of
Geneva, as nobody would deny.  Begun so languidly and
with such a fumbling hand that the first twenty pages or
more had to be thrown into the waste-paper basket,
*A Smile of Fortune*, the most purely Indian Ocean story
of the three, has ended by becoming what the reader will
see.  I will only say for myself that I have been patted on
the back for it by most unexpected people, personally
unknown to me, the chief of them of course being the
editor of a popular illustrated magazine who published
it serially in one mighty instalment.  Who will dare say
after this that the change of air had not been an immense
success ?

The origins of the middle story, *The Secret Sharer*,
are quite other.  It was written much earlier and was
published first in *Harper's Magazine*, during the early part,
I think, of 1911.  Or perhaps the latter part ?  My
memory on that point is hazy.  The basic fact of the
tale I had in my possession for a good many years.  It
was in truth the common possession of the whole fleet of
merchant ships trading to India, China, and Australia: a
great company the last years of which coincided with my
first years on the wider seas.  The fact itself happened
on board a very distinguished member of it, *Cutty Sark*
by name and belonging to Mr. Willis, a notable ship-
owner in his day, one of the kind (they are all underground
now) who used personally to see his ships start on their
voyages to those distant shores where they showed worthily

the honoured house-flag of their owner. I am glad I was not too late to get at least one glimpse of Mr. Willis on a very wet and gloomy morning watching from the pier head of the New South Dock one of his clippers starting on a China voyage—an imposing figure of a man under the invariable white hat so well known in the Port of London, waiting till the head of his ship had swung downstream before giving her a dignified wave of a big gloved hand. For all I know it may have been the *Cutty Sark* herself, though certainly not on that fatal voyage. I do not know the date of the occurrence on which the scheme of *The Secret Sharer* is founded; it came to light an even got into newspapers about the middle eighties, though I had heard of it before, as it were privately, among the officers of the great wool fleet in which my first years in deep water were served. It came to light under circumstances dramatic enough, I think, but which have nothing to do with my story. In the more specially maritime part of my writings this bit of presentation may take its place as one of my two Calm-pieces. For, if there is to be any classification by subjects, I have done two Storm-pieces in *The Nigger of the 'Narcissus'* and in *Typhoon*; and two Calm-pieces: this one and *The Shadow-Line*, a book which belongs to a later period.

Notwithstanding their autobiographical form the above two stories are not the record of personal experience. Their quality, such as it is, depends on something larger if less precise: on the character, vision, and sentiment of the first twenty independent years of my life. And the same may be said of the *Freya of the Seven Isles*. I was considerably abused for writing that story on the ground of its cruelty, both in public prints and in private letters.

I remember one from a man in America who was quite furiously angry. He told me with curses and imprecations that I had no right to write such an abominable thing which, he said, had gratuitously and intolerably harrowed his feelings. It was a very interesting letter to read. Impressive too. I carried it for some days in my pocket. Had I the right? The sincerity of the anger impressed me. Had I the right? Had I really sinned as he said or was it only that man's madness? Yet there was a method in his fury. . . . I composed in my mind a violent reply, a reply of mild argument, a reply of lofty detachment; but they never got on paper in the end and I have forgotten their phrasing. The very letter of the angry man has got lost somehow; and nothing remains now but the pages of the story which I cannot recall and would not recall if I could.

But I am glad to think that the two women in this book: Alice, the sullen, passive victim of her fate, and the actively individual Freya, so determined to be the mistress of her own destiny, must have evoked some sympathies because of all my volumes of short stories this was the one for which there was the greatest immediate demand.

1920.                                           J. C.

# CHANCE

A Tale in Two Parts

*Published in* 1914

# CHANCE

*Chance* is one of my novels that shortly after having been begun were laid aside for a few months. Starting impetuously like a sanguine oarsman setting forth in the early morning I came very soon to a fork in the stream and found it necessary to pause and reflect seriously upon the direction I would take. Either presented to me equal fascinations, at least on the surface, and for that very reason my hesitation extended over many days. I floated in the calm water of pleasant speculation, between the diverging currents of conflicting impulses, with an agreeable but perfectly irrational conviction that neither of those currents would take me to destruction. My sympathies being equally divided and the two forces being equal it is perfectly obvious that nothing but mere chance influenced my decision in the end. It is a mighty force, that of mere chance; absolutely irresistible yet manifesting itself often in delicate forms, such for instance as the charm, true or illusory, of a human being. It is very difficult to put one's finger on the imponderable, but I may venture to say that it is Flora de Barral who is really responsible for this novel which relates, in fact, the story of her life.

At the crucial moment of my indecision Flora de Barral passed before me, but so swiftly that I failed at first to get hold of her. Though loth to give her up I didn't see the way of pursuit clearly and was on the point of becoming discouraged when my natural liking for Captain Anthony came to my assistance. I said to myself that if that man was so determined to embrace a 'wisp of mist' the best thing for me was to join him in that eminently practical and praiseworthy adventure. I simply followed Captain Anthony. Each of us was bent on capturing his own dream. The reader will be able to judge of our success.

Captain Anthony's determination led him a long and roundabout course and that is why this book is a long book. That the course was of my own choosing I will not deny. A critic had remarked that if I had selected another method of composition and taken a little more trouble the tale could have been told in about two hundred pages. I confess I do not perceive exactly the bearings of such criticism or even the use of such a remark. No doubt that by selecting a certain method and taking great pains the whole story might have been written out on a cigarette paper. For that matter, the whole history of mankind could be written thus if only approached with sufficient detachment. The history of men on this earth since the beginning of ages may be resumed in one phrase of infinite poignancy: They were born, they suffered, they died. . . . Yet it is a great tale! But in the infinitely minute stories about men and women it is my lot on earth to narrate I am not capable of such detachment.

What makes this book memorable to me apart from the natural sentiment one has for one's creation is the response it provoked. The general public responded largely, more largely perhaps than to any other book of mine, in the only way the general public can respond, that is by buying a certain number of copies. This gave me a considerable amount of pleasure, because what I

always feared most was drifting unconsciously into the
position of a writer for a limited coterie; a position which
would have been odious to me as throwing a doubt on
the soundness of my belief in the solidarity of all mankind
in simple ideas and in sincere emotions.   Regarded as a
manifestation of criticism (for it would be outrageous to
deny to the general public the possession of a critical
mind) the reception was very satisfactory.   I saw that
I had managed to please a certain number of minds busy
attending to their own very real affairs.   It is agreeable
to think one is able to please.   From the minds whose
business it is precisely to criticize such attempts to please,
this book received an amount of discussion and of a rather
searching analysis which not only satisfied that personal
vanity I share with the rest of mankind but reached my
deeper feelings and aroused my gratified interest.   The
undoubted sympathy informing the varied appreciations
of that book was, I love to think, a recognition of my good
faith in the pursuit of my art—the art of the novelist which
a distinguished French writer at the end of a successful
career complained of as being 'trop difficile'! It is indeed
*too* arduous in the sense that the effort must be invariably
so much greater than the possible achievement.   In that
sort of foredoomed task which is in its nature very lonely
also, sympathy is a precious thing.   It can make the most
severe criticism welcome.   To be told that better things
have been expected of one may be soothing in view of
how much better things one had expected from oneself
in this art which, in these days, is no longer justified by
the assumption, somewhere and somehow, of a didactic
purpose.
    I do not mean to hint that anybody had ever done me

the injury (I don't mean insult, I mean injury) of charging
a single one of my pages with didactic purpose.   But every
subject in the region of intellect and emotion must have
a morality of its own if it is treated at all sincerely; and
even the most artful of writers will give himself (and his
morality) away in about every third sentence.   The varied
shades of moral significance which have been discovered
in my writings are very numerous.   None of them, however, have provoked a hostile manifestation.   It may have
happened to me to sin against taste now and then, but
apparently I have never sinned against the basic feelings
and elementary convictions which make life possible to
the mass of mankind and, by establishing a standard of
judgment, set their idealism free to look for plainer ways,
for higher feelings, for deeper purposes.

I cannot say that any particular moral complexion has
been put on this novel but I do not think that anybody
had detected in it an evil intention.   And it is only for
their intentions that men can be held responsible.   The
ultimate effects of whatever they do are far beyond their
control.   In doing this book my intention was to interest
people in my vision of things, which is indissolubly allied
to the style in which it is expressed.   In other words I
wanted to write a certain amount of pages in prose, which,
strictly speaking, is my proper business.   I have attended
to it conscientiously with the hope of being entertaining
or at least not insufferably boring to my readers.   I cannot sufficiently insist upon the truth that when I sit down
to write my intentions are always blameless however
deplorable the ultimate effect of the act may turn out
to be.

1920.                                              J. C.

# WITHIN THE TIDES

## Tales

The Planter of Malata
The Partner
The Inn of the Two Witches
Because of the Dollars

*Published in* 1915

# WITHIN THE TIDES

The tales collected in this book have elicited on their appearance two utterances in the shape of comment and one distinctly critical charge. A reviewer observed that I liked to write of men who go to sea or live on lonely islands untrammelled by the pressure of worldly circumstances, because such characters allowed freer play to my imagination which in their case was only bounded by natural laws and the universal human conventions. There is a certain truth in this remark no doubt. It is only the suggestion of deliberate choice that misses its mark. I have not sought for special imaginative freedom or a larger play of fancy in my choice of characters and subjects. The nature of the knowledge, suggestions or hints used in my imaginative work has depended directly on the conditions of my active life. It depended more on contacts, and very slight contacts at that, than on actual experience; because my life as a matter of fact was far from being adventurous in itself. Even now when I look back on it with a certain regret (who would not regret his youth?) and positive affection, its colouring wears the sober hue of hard work and exacting calls of duty, things which in themselves are not much charged with a feeling of romance. If these things appeal strongly to me even in retrospect it is, I suppose, because the romantic feeling of reality was in me an inborn faculty. This in itself may be a curse but when disciplined by a sense of personal responsibility and a recognition of the hard facts of existence shared with the rest of mankind becomes but a point of view from which the very shadows of life appear endowed with an internal glow. And such romanticism is not a sin. It is none the worse for the knowledge of truth. It only tries to make the best of it, hard as it may be; and in this hardness discovers a certain aspect of beauty.

I am speaking here of romanticism in relation to life, not of romanticism in relation to imaginative literature, which, in its early days, was associated simply with medieval subjects, or, at any rate, with subjects sought for in a remote past. My subjects are not medieval and I have a natural right to them because my past is very much my own. If their course lie out of the beaten path of organized social life, it is, perhaps, because I myself did in a sort break away from it early in obedience to an impulse which must have been very genuine since it has sustained me through all the dangers of disillusion. But that origin of my literary work was very far from giving a larger scope to my imagination. On the contrary, the mere fact of dealing with matters outside the general run of everyday experience laid me under the obligation of a more scrupulous fidelity to the truth of my own sensations. The problem was to make unfamiliar things credible. To do that I had to create for them, to reproduce for them, to envelop them in their proper atmosphere of actuality. This was the hardest task of all and the most important, in view of that conscientious rendering of truth in thought and fact which has been always my aim.

The other utterance of the two I have alluded to above consisted in the observation that in this volume of mine the whole was greater than its parts. I pass it on to my

readers, merely remarking that if this is really so then
I must take it as a tribute to my personality, since those
stories which by implication seem to hold so well together
as to be surveyed *en bloc* and judged as the product of
a single mood, were written at different times, under
various influences, and with the deliberate intention of
trying several ways of telling a tale.   The hints and
suggestions for all of them had been received at various
times and in distant parts of the globe.   The book received
a good deal of varied criticism, mainly quite justifiable,
but in a couple of instances quite surprising in its objec-
tions.   Amongst them was the critical charge of false
realism brought against the opening story, *The Planter
of Malata*.   I would have regarded it as serious enough
if I had not discovered on reading further that the distinguished critic was accusing me simply of having sought
to evade a happy ending out of a sort of moral cowardice,
lest I should be condemned as a superficially sentimental
person.   Where (and of what sort) there are to be found
in *The Planter of Malata* any germs of happiness that
could have fructified at the end I am at a loss to see.
Such criticism seems to miss the whole purpose and significance of a piece of writing the primary intention of
which was mainly aesthetic; an essay in description and
narrative around a given psychological situation.   Of more
seriousness was the spoken criticism of an old and valued
friend who thought that in the scene near the rock, which
from the point of view of psychology is crucial, neither
Felicia Moorsom nor Goeffrey Renouard find the right
things to say to each other.   I didn't argue the point at
the time, for, to be candid, I didn't feel quite satisfied
with the scene myself.   On re-reading it lately for the

purpose of this edition, I have come to the conclusion that there is that much truth in my friend's criticism that I have made those people a little too explicit in their emotion and thus have destroyed to a certain extent the characteristic illusory glamour of their personalities. I regret this defect very much, for I regard *The Planter of Malata* as a nearly successful attempt at doing a very difficult thing which I would have liked to have made as perfect as it lay in my power. Yet considering the pitch and the tonality of the whole tale it is very difficult to imagine what else those two people could have found to say at that time and on that particular spot of the earth's surface. In the mood in which they both were, and given the exceptional state of their feelings, anything might have been said.

The eminent critic who charged me with false realism, the outcome of timidity, was quite wrong. I should like to ask him what he imagines the, so to speak, lifelong embrace of Felicia Moorsom and Geoffrey Renouard could have been like? Could it have been at all? Would it have been credible? No! I did not shirk anything, either from timidity or laziness. Perhaps a little mistrust of my own powers would not have been altogether out of place in this connection. But it failed me; and I resemble Geoffrey Renouard in so far that when once engaged in an adventure I cannot bear the idea of turning back. The moment had arrived for these people to disclose themselves. They had to do it. To render a crucial point of feelings in terms of human speech is really an impossible task. Written words can only form a sort of translation. And if that translation happens, from want of skill or from over-anxiety, to be too literal, the people

caught in the toils of passion, instead of disclosing themselves, which would be art, are made to give themselves
away, which is neither art nor life. Nor yet truth! At
any rate, not the whole truth; for it is truth robbed of all
its necessary and sympathetic reservations and qualifica-
tions which give it its fair form, its just proportions, its
semblance of human fellowship.

Indeed the task of the translator of passions into speech
may be pronounced 'too difficult.' However, with my
customary impenitence I am glad I have attempted the
story with all its implications and difficulties, including
the scene by the side of the grey rock crowning the
height of Malata. But I am not so inordinately pleased
with the result as not to be able to forgive a patient
reader who may find it somewhat disappointing.

I have left myself no space to talk about the other three
stories because I do not think that they call for detailed
comment. Each of them has its special mood and I have
tried purposely to give each its special tone and a different
construction of phrase. A reviewer asked in reference
to *The Inn of the Two Witches* whether I ever came
across a tale called 'A Very Strange Bed' published in
*Household Words* in 1852 or '54. I never saw a number
of *Household Words* of that decade. A bed of the sort
was discovered in an inn on the road between Rome and
Naples at the end of the eighteenth century. Where
I picked up the information I cannot say now, but I am
certain it was not in a tale. This bed is the only 'fact'
of *The Witches' Inn*. The other two stories have considerably more 'fact' in them, derived from my own
personal knowledge.

1920.                                              J. C.

# VICTORY

## An Island Tale

*Published in* 1915

# VICTORY

On approaching the task of writing this Note for *Victory* the first thing I am conscious of is the actual nearness of the book, its nearness to me personally, to the vanished mood in which it was written and to the mixed feelings aroused by the critical notices the book obtained when first published almost exactly a year after the beginning of the Great War. The writing of it was finished in 1914 long before the murder of an Austrian archduke sounded the first note of warning for a world already full of doubts and fears.

The contemporaneous very short Author's Note which is preserved in this edition[1] bears sufficient witness to the feelings with which I consented to the publication of the book. The fact of the book having been published in the United States early in the year made it difficult to delay its appearance in England any longer. It came out in the thirteenth month of the War, and my conscience was troubled by the awful incongruity of throwing this bit of imagined drama into the welter of reality, tragic enough in all conscience but even more cruel than tragic and more inspiring than cruel. It seemed awfully presumptuous to think there would be eyes to spare for those pages in a community which in the crash of the big guns and in the din of brave words expressing the truth of an indomitable faith could not but feel the edge of a sharp knife at its throat.

1 See Appendix, page 211.

The unchanging Man of history is wonderfully adaptable both by his power of endurance and in his capacity for detachment. The fact seems to be that the play of his destiny is too great for his fears and too mysterious for his understanding. Were the trump of the Last Judgment to sound suddenly on a working day the musician at his piano would go on with his performance of Beethoven's sonata and the cobbler at his stall stick to his last in undisturbed confidence in the virtues of the leather. And with perfect propriety. For what are we to let ourselves be disturbed by an angel's vengeful music too mighty for our ears and too awful for our terrors? Thus it happens to us to be struck suddenly by the lightning of wrath. The reader will go on reading if the book pleases him and the critic will go on criticizing with that faculty of detachment born perhaps from a sense of infinite littleness and which is yet the only faculty that seems to assimilate man to the immortal gods.

It is only when the catastrophe matches the natural obscurity of our fate that even the best representative of the race is liable to lose his detachment. It is very obvious that on the arrival of the gentlemanly Mr. Jones, the single-minded Ricardo and the faithful Pedro, Heyst, the man of universal detachment, loses his mental self-possession, that fine attitude before the universally irremediable which wears the name of stoicism. It is all a matter of proportion. There should have been a remedy for that sort of thing. And yet there is no remedy. Behind this minute instance of life's hazards Heyst sees the power of blind destiny. Besides, Heyst in his fine detachment had lost the habit of asserting himself. I don't mean the courage of self-assertion, either moral or physical, but

the mere way of it, the trick of the thing, the readiness
of mind and the turn of the hand that come without
reflection and lead the man to excellence in life, in art,
in crime, in virtue, and for the matter of that, even in
love. Thinking is the great enemy of perfection. The
habit of profound reflection, I am compelled to say,
is the most pernicious of all the habits formed by the
civilized man.

But I wouldn't be suspected even remotely of making
fun of Axel Heyst. I have always liked him. The flesh
and blood individual who stands behind the infinitely more
familiar figure of the book I remember as a mysterious
Swede right enough. Whether he was a baron, too, I
am not so certain. He himself never laid a claim to that
distinction. His detachment was too great to make any
claims, big or small, on one's credulity. I will not say
where I met him because I fear to give my readers a wrong
impression, since a marked incongruity between a man
and his surroundings is often a very misleading circumstance. We became very friendly for a time and I would
not like to expose him to unpleasant suspicions though,
personally, I am sure he would have been indifferent
to suspicions as he was indifferent to all the other dis-
advantages of life. He was not the whole Heyst of course;
he is only the physical and moral foundation of my Heyst
laid on the ground of a short acquaintance. That it was
short was certainly not my fault for he had charmed me
by the mere amenity of his detachment which, in this
case, I cannot help thinking he had carried to excess.
He went away from his rooms without leaving a trace.
I wondered where he had gone to—but now I know.
He vanished from my ken only to drift into this adventure

that, unavoidable, waited for him in a world which he persisted in looking upon as a malevolent shadow spinning in the sunlight. Often in the course of years an expressed sentiment, the particular sense of a phrase heard casually, would recall him to my mind so that I have fastened on to him many words heard on other men's lips and belonging to other men's less perfect, less pathetic moods.

The same observation will apply *mutatis mutandis* to Mr. Jones, who is built on a much slenderer connection. Mr. Jones (or whatever his name was) did not drift away from me. He turned his back on me and walked out of the room. It was in a little hotel in the island of St. Thomas in the West Indies (in the year '75) where we found him one hot afternoon extended on three chairs, all alone in the loud buzzing of flies to which his immobility and his cadaverous aspect gave a most gruesome significance. Our invasion must have displeased him because he got off the chairs brusquely and walked out, leaving with me an indelibly weird impression of his thin shanks. One of the men with me said that the fellow was the most desperate gambler he had ever come across. I said: 'A professional sharper?' and got for answer: 'He's a terror; but I must say that up to a certain point he will play fair. . . .' I wonder what the point was. I never saw him again because I believe he went straight on board a mail-boat which left within the hour for other ports of call in the direction of Aspinall. Mr. Jones's characteristic insolence belongs to another man of a quite different type. I will say nothing as to the origins of his mentality because I don't intend to make any damaging admissions.

It so happened that the very same year Ricardo—the physical Ricardo—was a fellow-passenger of mine on board

an extremely small and extremely dirty little schooner,
during a four days' passage between two places in the
Gulf of Mexico whose names don't matter.   For the most
part he lay on deck aft as it were at my feet, and raising
himself from time to time on his elbow would talk about
himself and go on talking, not exactly to me or even at
me (he would not even look up but kept his eyes fixed
on the deck) but more as if communing in a low voice
with his familiar devil.   Now and then he would give me
a glance and make the hairs of his stiff little moustache
stir quaintly.   His eyes were green and every cat I see
to this day reminds me of the exact contour of his face.
What he was travelling for or what was his business in
life he never confided to me.   Truth to say, the only
passenger on board that schooner who could have talked
openly about his activities and purposes was a very snuffy
and conversationally delightful friar, the Superior of a
convent, attended by a very young lay brother, of a particularly ferocious countenance.   We had with us also,
lying prostrate in the dark and unspeakable cuddy of that
schooner, an old Spanish gentleman, owner of much
luggage and, as Ricardo assured me, very ill indeed.
Ricardo seemed to be either a servant or the confidant of
that aged and distinguished-looking invalid, who early on
the passage held a long murmured conversation with the
friar, and after that did nothing but groan feebly, smoke
cigarettes, and now and then call for Martin in a voice
full of pain.   Then he who has become Ricardo in the
book would go below into that beastly and noisome hole,
remain there mysteriously, and coming up on deck again
with a face on which nothing could be read, would as
likely as not resume for my edification the exposition of

his moral attitude toward life illustrated by striking particular instances of the most atrocious complexion.   Did
he mean to frighten me?   Or seduce me?   Or astonish
me?   Or arouse my admiration?   All he did was to
arouse my amused incredulity.   As scoundrels go he was
far from being a bore.   For the rest my innocence was so
great then that I could not take his philosophy seriously.
All the time he kept one ear turned to the cuddy in the
manner of a devoted servant, but I had the idea that in
some way or other he had imposed the connection on the
invalid for some end of his own.   The reader, therefore,
won't be surprised to hear that one morning I was told
without any particular emotion by the *padrone* of the
schooner that the 'rich man' down there was dead: he
had died in the night.   I don't remember ever being
so moved by the desolate end of a complete stranger.
I looked down the skylight and there was the devoted
Martin busy cording cowhide trunks belonging to the
deceased, whose white beard and hooked nose were the
only parts I could make out in the dark depths of a
horrible, stuffy bunk.

As it fell calm in the course of the afternoon and continued calm during all that night and the terrible, flaming
day, the late 'rich man' had to be thrown overboard at
sunset, though as a matter of fact we were in sight of the
low, pestilential, mangrove-lined coast of our destination.
The excellent Father Superior mentioned to me with
an air of immense commiseration: 'The poor man has
left a young daughter.'   Who was to look after her I
don't know, but I saw the devoted Martin taking the
trunks ashore with great care just before I landed myself.
I would perhaps have tracked the ways of that man

of immense sincerity for a little while, but I had some of my own very pressing business to attend to, which in the end got mixed up with an earthquake, and so I had no time to give to Ricardo. The reader need not be told that I have not forgotten him, though.

My contact with the faithful Pedro was much shorter and my observation of him was less complete but incomparably more anxious. It ended in a sudden inspiration to get out of his way. It was in a hovel of sticks and mats by the side of a path. As I went in there only to ask for a bottle of lemonade I have not to this day the slightest idea what in my appearance or actions could have roused his terrible ire. It became manifest to me less than two minutes after I had set eyes on him for the first time, and though immensely surprised of course I didn't stop to think it out. I took the nearest short cut through the wall. This beotial apparition, and a certain enormous buck nigger encountered in Haiti only a couple of months afterwards, have fixed my conception of blind, furious, unreasoning rage, as manifested in the human animal, to the end of my days. Of the nigger I used to dream for years afterwards. Of Pedro never. The impression was less vivid. I got away from him too quickly.

It seems to me but natural that those three buried in a corner of my memory should suddenly get out into the light of the world—so natural that I offer no excuse for their existence. They were there, they had to come out; and this is a sufficient excuse for a writer of tales who had taken to his trade without preparation, or premeditation, and without any moral intention but that which pervades the whole scheme of this world of senses.

M

Since this Note is mostly concerned with personal contacts and the origins of the persons in the tale, I am bound
also to speak of Lena, because if I were to leave her out
it would look like a slight; and nothing would be further
from my thoughts than putting a slight on Lena. If of
all the personages involved in the 'mystery of Samburan'
I have lived longest with Heyst (or with him I call Heyst)
it was at her, whom I call Lena, that I have looked the
longest and with a most sustained attention. This attention originated in idleness, for which I have a natural
talent. One evening I wandered into a café, in a town
not of the tropics but of the south of France. It was
filled with tobacco smoke, the hum of voices, the rattling
of dominoes, and the sounds of strident music. The
orchestra was rather smaller than the one that performed
at Schomberg's hotel, had the air more of a family party
than of an enlisted band, and, I must confess, seemed
rather more respectable than the Zangiacomo musical
enterprise. It was less pretentious also, more homely
and familiar, so to speak, insomuch that in the intervals
when all the performers left the platform one of them
went amongst the marble tables collecting offerings of
sous and francs in a battered tin receptacle recalling the
shape of a sauceboat. It was a girl. Her detachment
from her task seems to me now to have equalled or even
surpassed Heyst's aloofness from all the mental degrada-
tions to which a man's intelligence is exposed in its way
through life. Silent and wide-eyed she went from table
to table with the air of a sleep-walker and with no other
sound but the slight rattle of the coins to attract attention.
It was long after the sea-chapter of my life had been
closed but it is difficult to discard completely the charac-

teristics of half a lifetime, and it was in something of the
Jack-ashore spirit that I dropped a five-franc piece into
the sauceboat; whereupon the sleep-walker turned her
head to gaze at me and said 'Merci, monsieur,' in a tone in
which there was no gratitude but only surprise.  I must
have been idle indeed to take the trouble to remark on
such slight evidence that the voice was very charming
and when the performers resumed their seats I shifted my
position slightly in order not to have that particular per-
former hidden from me by the little man with the beard
who conducted, and who might for all I know have been
her father, but whose real mission in life was to be a
model for the Zangiacomo of *Victory*.  Having got a clear
line of sight I naturally (being idle) continued to look at
the girl through all the second part of the programme.
The shape of her dark head inclined over the violin
was fascinating, and, while resting between the pieces of
that interminable programme, she was, in her white dress
and with her brown hands reposing in her lap, the very
image of dreamy innocence.  The mature, bad-tempered
woman at the piano might have been her mother, though
there was not the slightest resemblance between them.
All I am certain of in their personal relation to each other
is that cruel pinch on the upper part of the arm.  That
I am sure I have seen!  There could be no mistake.
I was in a too idle mood to imagine such a gratuitous bar-
barity.  It may have been playfulness, yet the girl jumped
up as if she had been stung by a wasp.  It may have been
playfulness.  Yet I saw plainly poor 'dreamy innocence'
rub gently the affected place as she filed off with the other
performers down the middle aisle between the marble
tables in the uproar of voices, the rattling of dominoes,

through a blue atmosphere of tobacco smoke. I believe that those people left the town next day.

Or perhaps they had only migrated to the other big café, on the other side of the Place de la Comédie. It is very possible. I did not go across to find out. It was my perfect idleness that had invested the girl with a peculiar charm, and I did not want to destroy it by any superfluous exertion. The receptivity of my indolence made the impression so permanent that when the moment came for her meeting with Heyst I felt that she would be heroically equal to every demand of the risky and uncertain future. I was so convinced of it that I let her go with Heyst, I won't say without a pang but certainly without misgivings. And in view of her triumphant end what more could I have done for her rehabilitation and her happiness?

1920.                                                J. C.

# THE SHADOW-LINE

A Confession

*Published in* 1917

# THE SHADOW-LINE

This story, which I admit to be in its brevity a fairly complex piece of work, was not intended to touch on the supernatural. Yet more than one critic has been inclined to take it in that way, seeing in it an attempt on my part to give the fullest scope to my imagination by taking it beyond the confines of the world of the living, suffering humanity. But as a matter of fact my imagination is not made of stuff so elastic as all that. I believe that if I attempted to put the strain of the supernatural on it it would fail deplorably and exhibit an unlovely gap. But I could never have attempted such a thing, because all my moral and intellectual being is penetrated by an invincible conviction that whatever falls under the dominion of our senses must be in nature and, however exceptional, cannot differ in its essence from all the other effects of the visible and tangible world of which we are a self-conscious part. The world of the living contains enough marvels and mysteries as it is; marvels and mysteries acting upon our emotions and intelligence in ways so inexplicable that it would almost justify the conception of life as an enchanted state. No, I am too firm in my consciousness of the marvellous to be ever fascinated by the mere supernatural, which (take it any way you like) is but a manufactured article, the fabrication of minds insensitive to the intimate delicacies of our relation to the dead and to the living, in their countless multitudes; a desecration of our tenderest memories; an outrage on our dignity.

Whatever my native modesty may be it will never condescend so low as to seek help for my imagination within those vain imaginings common to all ages and that in themselves are enough to fill all lovers of mankind with unutterable sadness.    As to the effect of a mental or moral shock on a common mind, that is quite a legitimate subject for study and description.    Mr. Burns's moral being receives a severe shock in his relations with his late captain, and this in his diseased state turns into a mere superstitious fancy compounded of fear and animosity. This fact is one of the elements of the story, but there is nothing supernatural in it, nothing so to speak from beyond the confines of this world, which in all conscience holds enough mystery and terror in itself.

Perhaps if I had published this tale, which I have had for a long time in my mind, under the title of 'First Command' no suggestion of the supernatural would have been found in it by any impartial reader, critical or otherwise.    I will not consider here the origins of the feeling in which its actual title, *The Shadow-Line*, occurred to my mind.    Primarily the aim of this piece of writing was the presentation of certain facts which certainly were associated with the change from youth, care-free and fervent, to the more self-conscious and more poignant period of maturer life.    Nobody can doubt that before the supreme trial of a whole generation I had an acute consciousness of the minute and insignificant character of my own obscure experience.    There could be no question here of any parallelism.    That notion never entered my head.    But there was a feeling of identity, though with an enormous difference of scale—as of one single drop measured against the bitter and stormy immensity of an ocean. And this was very natural too. For when we begin to meditate on the meaning of our own past it seems to fill all the world in its profundity and its magnitude. This book was written in the last three months of the year 1916. Of all the subjects of which a writer of tales is more or less conscious within himself this is the only one I found it possible to attempt at the time. The depth and the nature of the mood with which I approached it is best expressed perhaps in the dedication, which strikes me now as a most disproportionate thing—as another instance of the overwhelming greatness of our own emotion to ourselves.

This much having been said I may pass on now to a few remarks about the mere material of the story. As to locality it belongs to that part of the Eastern Seas from which I have carried away into my writing life the greatest number of suggestions. From my statement that I thought of this story for a long time under the title of 'First Command' the reader may guess that it is concerned with my personal experience. And as a matter of fact it *is* personal experience seen in perspective with the eye of the mind and coloured by that affection one can't help feeling for such events of one's life as one has no reason to be ashamed of. And that affection is as intense (I appeal here to universal experience) as the shame, and almost the anguish with which one remembers some unfortunate occurrences, down to mere mistakes in speech, that have been perpetrated by one in the past. The effect of perspective in memory is to make things loom large because the essentials stand out isolated from their surroundings of insignificant daily facts which have naturally faded out of one's mind. I remember that period of my sea-life with pleasure because, begun inauspiciously, it turned out in the end a success from a personal point of view, leaving a tangible proof in the terms of the letter the owners of the ship wrote to me two years afterwards when I resigned my command in order to come home. This resignation marked the beginning of another phase of my seaman's life, its terminal phase, if I may say so, which in its own way has coloured another portion of my writings.   I didn't know then how near its end my sea-life was, and therefore I felt no sorrow except at parting with the ship.   I was sorry also to break my connection with the firm which owned her and who were pleased to receive with friendly kindness and give their confidence to a man who had entered their service in an accidental manner and in very adverse circumstances. Without disparaging the earnestness of my purpose I suspect now that luck had no small part in the success of the trust reposed in me.   And one cannot help re-membering with pleasure the time when one's best efforts were seconded by a run of luck.

The words 'Worthy of my undying regard' selected by me for the motto on the title-page are quoted from the text of the book itself; and, though one of my critics surmised that they applied to the ship, it is evident from the place where they stand that they refer to the men of that ship's company: complete strangers to their new captain and yet who stood by him so well during those twenty days that seemed to have been passed on the brink of a slow and agonizing destruction. And *that* is the greatest memory of all! For surely it is a great thing to have commanded a hand-ful of men worthy of one's undying regard.

1920.                                          J. C.

# THE ARROW OF GOLD

A Story between Two Notes

*Published in* 1919

# THE ARROW OF GOLD

Having named all the short prefaces written for my books, Author's Notes, this one too must have the same heading for the sake of uniformity if at the risk of some confusion. *The Arrow of Gold*, as its sub-title states, is a story between two Notes. But these Notes are embodied in its very frame, belong to its texture, and their mission is to prepare and close the story. They are material to the comprehension of the experience related in the narrative and are meant to determine the time and place together with certain historical circumstances conditioning the existence of the people concerned in the transactions of the twelve months covered by the narrative. It was the shortest way of getting over the preliminaries of a piece of work which could not have been of the nature of a chronicle.

*The Arrow of Gold* is my first after-the-War publication. The writing of it was begun in the autumn of 1917 and finished in the summer of 1918. Its memory is associated with that of the darkest hour of the War, which, in accordance with the well-known proverb—preceded the dawn—the dawn of peace.

As I look at them now, these pages, written in the days of stress and dread, wear a look of strange serenity. They were written calmly, yet not in cold blood, and are perhaps the only kind of pages I could have written at that time full of menace, but also full of faith.

The subject of this book I had been carrying about

with me for many years, not so much a possession of my
memory as an inherent part of myself. It was ever present
to my mind and ready to my hand, but I was loth to touch
it, from a feeling of what I imagined to be mere shyness
but which in reality was a very comprehensible mistrust
of myself.

In plucking the fruit of memory one runs the risk of
spoiling its bloom, especially if it has got to be carried
into the market-place. This being the product of my
private garden my reluctance can be easily understood;
and though some critics have expressed their regret that
I had not written this book fifteen years earlier I do not
share that opinion. If I took it up so late in life it is
because the right moment had not arrived till then.
I mean the positive feeling of it, which is a thing that
cannot be discussed. Neither will I discuss here the
regrets of those critics, which seem to me the most
irrelevant thing that could have been said in connection
with literary criticism.

I never tried to conceal the origins of the subject-
matter of this book which I have hesitated so long to write;
but some reviewers indulged themselves with a sense of
triumph in discovering in it my Dominic of *The Mirror
of the Sea* under his own name (a truly wonderful discovery) and in recognizing the *balancelle Tremolino* in the
unnamed little craft in which Mr. George plied his fantastic trade and sought to allay the pain of his incurable
wound. I am not in the least disconcerted by this display
of perspicacity. It is the same man and the same balancelle. But for the purposes of a book like *The Mirror of
the Sea* all I could make use of was the personal history of
the little *Tremolino*. The present work is not in any sense

an attempt to develop a subject lightly touched upon in former years and in connection with quite another kind of love.   What the story of the *Tremolino* in its anecdotic character has in common with the story of *The Arrow of Gold* is the quality of initiation (through an ordeal which required some resolution to face) into the life of passion. In the few pages at the end of *The Mirror of the Sea* and in the whole volume of *The Arrow of Gold*, *that* and no other is the subject offered to the public.   The pages and the book form together a complete record; and the only assurance I can give my readers is, that as it stands here with all its imperfections it is given to them complete.

I venture this explicit statement because, amidst much sympathetic appreciation, I have detected here and there a note, as it were, of suspicion.   Suspicion of facts concealed, of explanations held back, of inadequate motives. But what is lacking in the facts is simply what I did not know, and what is not explained is what I did not understand myself, and what seems inadequate is the fault of my imperfect insight.   And all that I could not help. In the case of this book I was unable to supplement these deficiencies by the exercise of my inventive faculty.   It was never very strong; and on this occasion its use would have seemed exceptionally dishonest.   It is from that ethical motive and not from timidity that I elected to keep strictly within the limits of unadorned sincerity and to try to enlist the sympathies of my readers without assuming lofty omniscience or descending to the subterfuge of exaggerated emotions.

1920.                                        J. C.

# THE RESCUE

A Romance of the Shallows

*Published in* 1920

# THE RESCUE

Of the three long novels of mine which suffered an interruption, *The Rescue* was the one that had to wait the longest for the good pleasure of the Fates. I am betraying no secret when I state here that it had to wait precisely for twenty years. I laid it aside at the end of the summer of 1898 and it was about the end of the summer of 1918 that I took it up again with the firm determination to see the end of it and helped by the sudden feeling that I might be equal to the task.

This does not mean that I turned to it with elation. I was well aware and perhaps even too much aware of the dangers of such an adventure. The amazingly sympathetic kindness which men of various temperaments, diverse views, and different literary tastes have been for years displaying towards my work has done much for me, has done all—except giving me that overweening self-confidence which may assist an adventurer sometimes but in the long run ends by leading him to the gallows.

As the characteristic I want most to impress upon these short Author's Notes prepared for my first Collected Edition is that of absolute frankness, I hasten to declare that I founded my hopes not on my supposed merits but on the continued goodwill of my readers. I may say at once that my hopes have been justified out of all proportion to my deserts. I met with the most considerate, most delicately expressed criticism free from all antagonism and in its conclusions showing an insight which in

itself could not fail to move me deeply, but was associated
also with enough commendation to make me feel rich
beyond the dreams of avarice—I mean an artist's avarice
which seeks its treasure in the hearts of men and women.

No! Whatever the preliminary anxieties might have
been this adventure was not to end in sorrow. Once
more Fortune favoured audacity; and yet I have never
forgotten the jocular translation of *Audaces fortuna juvat*
offered to me by my tutor when I was a small boy: 'The
audacious get bitten.' However, he took care to mention
that there were various kinds of audacity. Oh, there are,
there are! . . . There is, for instance, the kind of
audacity almost indistinguishable from impudence. . . .
I must believe that in this case I have not been impudent
for I am not conscious of having been bitten.

The truth is that when *The Rescue* was laid aside it was
not laid aside in despair. Several reasons contributed to
this abandonment and, no doubt, the first of them was
the growing sense of general difficulty in the handling of
the subject. The contents and the course of the story
I had clearly in my mind. But as to the way of presenting
the facts, and perhaps in a certain measure as to the nature
of the facts themselves, I had many doubts. I mean the
telling, representative facts, helpful to carry on the idea,
and, at the same time, of such a nature as not to demand
an elaborate creation of the atmosphere to the detriment
of the action. I did not see how I could avoid becoming
wearisome in the presentation of detail and in the pursuit
of clearness. I saw the action plainly enough. What
I had lost for the moment was the sense of the proper
formula of expression, the only formula that would suit.
This, of course, weakened my confidence in the intrinsic

worth and in the possible interest of the story—that is, in my invention. But I suspect that all the trouble was, in reality, the doubt of my prose, the doubt of its adequacy, of its power to master both the colours and the shades.

It is difficult to describe, exactly as I remember it, the complex state of my feelings; but those of my readers who take an interest in artistic perplexities will understand me best when I point out that I dropped *The Rescue* not to give myself up to idleness, regrets, or dreaming, but to begin *The Nigger of the 'Narcissus'* and to go on with it without hesitation and without a pause. A comparison of any page of *The Rescue* with any page of *The Nigger* will furnish an ocular demonstration of the nature and the inward meaning of this first crisis of my writing life. For it was a crisis undoubtedly. The laying aside of a work so far advanced was a very awful decision to take. It was wrung from me by a sudden conviction that *there* only was the road of salvation, the clear way out for an uneasy conscience. The finishing of *The Nigger* brought to my troubled mind the comforting sense of an accomplished task, and the first consciousness of a certain sort of mastery which could accomplish something with the aid of propitious stars. Why I did not return to *The Rescue* at once then, was not for the reason that I had grown afraid of it. Being able now to assume a firm attitude I said to myself deliberately: 'That thing can wait.' At the same time I was just as certain in my mind that *Youth*, a story which I had then, so to speak, on the tip of my pen, could *not* wait. Neither could *Heart of Darkness* be put off; for the practical reason that Mr. Wm. Blackwood having requested me to write something for the No. M of his magazine I had to stir up at once the subject

of that tale which had been long lying quiescent in my
mind; because, obviously, the venerable *Maga* at her
patriarchal age of 1,000 numbers could not be kept
waiting.    Then *Lord Jim*, with about seventeen pages
already written at odd times, put in his claim which was
irresistible.    Thus every stroke of the pen was taking me
further away from the abandoned *Rescue*, not without some
compunction on my part but with a gradually diminishing
resistance; till at last I let myself go, as if recognizing
a superior influence against which it was useless to
contend.

The years passed and the pages grew in number, and the
long reveries of which they were the outcome stretched
wide between me and the deserted *Rescue* like the smooth
hazy spaces of a dreamy sea.    Yet I never actually lost
sight of that dark speck in the misty distance.    It had
grown very small but it asserted itself with the appeal of
old associations.    It seemed to me that it would be a base
thing for me to slip out of the world leaving it out there
all alone, waiting for its fate—that would never come!

Sentiment, pure sentiment as you see, prompted me in
the last instance to face the pains and hazards of that
return.    As I moved slowly towards the abandoned body
of the tale it loomed up big amongst the glittering shallows
of the coast, lonely but not forbidding.    There was
nothing about it of a grim derelict.    It had an air of
expectant life.    One after another I made out the familiar
faces watching my approach with faint smiles of amused
recognition.    They had known well enough that I was
bound to come back to them.    But their eyes met mine
seriously, as was only to be expected since I, myself, felt
very serious as I stood amongst them again after years of

absence.    At once, without wasting words, we went to
work together on our renewed life; and every moment
I felt more strongly that They Who had Waited bore no
grudge to the man who, however widely he may have
wandered at times, had played truant only once in his life.

1920.                                                    J. C.

# NOTES ON LIFE AND LETTERS

*Published in* 1921

# NOTES ON LIFE AND LETTERS

I don't know whether I ought to offer an apology for this collection, which has more to do with life than with letters. Its appeal is made to orderly minds. This, to be frank about it, is a process of tidying up, which, from the nature of things, cannot be regarded as premature. The fact is that I wanted to do it myself because of a feeling that had nothing to do with the considerations of worthiness or unworthiness of the small (but unbroken) pieces collected within the covers of this volume. Of course it may be said that I might have taken up a broom and used it without saying anything about it. That, certainly, is one way of tidying up.

But it would have been too much to have expected me to treat all this matter as removable rubbish. All those things had a place in my life. Whether any of them deserve to have been picked up and ranged on the shelf —this shelf—I cannot say, and, frankly, I have not allowed my mind to dwell on the question. I was afraid of thinking myself into a mood that would hurt my feelings; for those pieces of writing, whatever may be the comment on their display, appertain to the character of the man.

And so here they are, dusted, which was but a decent thing to do, but in no way polished, extending from the the year '98 to the year '20, a thin array (for such a stretch of time) of really innocent attitudes: Conrad literary, Conrad political, Conrad reminiscent, Conrad controversial. Well, yes! A one-man show—or is it merely the show of one man?

The only thing that will not be found amongst those Figures and Things that have passed away, will be Conrad *en pantoufles.* It is a constitutional inability. *Schlafrock und Pantoffeln!* Not that! Never! . . . I don't know whether I dare boast like a certain South American general who used to say that no emergency of war or peace had ever found him 'with his boots off'; but I may say that whenever the various periodicals mentioned in this book called on me to come out and blow the trumpet of personal opinions or strike the pensive lute that speaks of the past, I always tried to pull on my boots first. I didn't want to do it, God knows! Their editors, to whom I beg to offer my thanks here, made me perform mainly by kindness but partly by bribery. Well, yes! Bribery. What can you expect? I never pretended to be better than the people in the next street or even in the same street.

This volume (including these embarrassed introductory remarks) is as near as I shall ever come to *déshabillé* in public; and perhaps it will do something to help towards a better vision of the man, if it gives no more than a partial view of a piece of his back, a little dusty (after the process of tidying up), a little bowed, and receding from the world not because of weariness or misanthropy but for other reasons that cannot be helped: because the leaves fall, the water flows, the clock ticks with that horrid pitiless solemnity which you must have observed in the ticking of the hall clock at home. For reasons like that. Yes! It recedes. And this was the chance to afford one more view of it—even to my own eyes.

The section within this volume called Letters explains itself, though I do not pretend to say that it justifies its own existence. It claims nothing in its defence except the right of speech which I believe belongs to everybody outside a Trappist monastery. The part I have ventured, for shortness' sake, to call Life, may perhaps justify itself by the emotional sincerity of the feelings to which the various papers included under that head owe their origin. And as they relate to events of which every one has a date, they are in the nature of signposts pointing out the direction my thoughts were compelled to take at the various cross-roads. If anybody detects any sort of consistency in the choice this will be only proof positive that wisdom had nothing to do with it. Whether right or wrong, instinct alone is invariable; a fact which only adds a deeper shade to its inherent mystery. The appearance of intellectuality these pieces may present at first sight is merely the result of the arrangement of words. The logic that may be found there is only the logic of the language. But I need not labour the point. There will be plenty of people sagacious enough to perceive the absence of all wisdom from these pages. But I believe sufficiently in human sympathies to imagine that very few will question their sincerity. Whatever delusions I may have suffered from I have had no delusions as to the nature of the facts commented on here. I may have misjudged their import: but that is the sort of error for which one may expect a certain amount of toleration.

The only paper of this collection which has never been published before is the Note on the Polish Problem. It was written at the request of a friend to be shown privately, and its 'Protectorate' idea, sprung from a strong sense of the critical nature of the situation, was shaped by the actual circumstances of the time. The time was about a month before the entrance of Roumania into the war, and though, honestly, I had seen already the shadow of coming events I could not permit my misgivings to enter into and destroy the structure of my plan. I still believe that there was some sense in it. It may certainly be charged with the appearance of lack of faith and it lays itself open to the throwing of many stones; but my object was practical and I had to consider warily the preconceived notions of the people to whom it was implicitly addressed and also their unjustifiable hopes. They were unjustifiable, but who was to tell them that? I mean who was wise enough and convincing enough to show them the inanity of their mental attitude? The whole atmosphere was poisoned with visions that were not so much false as simply impossible. They were also the result of vague and unconfessed fears, and that made their strength. For myself, with a very definite dread in my heart, I was careful not to allude to their character because I did not want the Note to be thrown away unread. And then I had to remember that the impossible has sometimes the trick of coming to pass, to the confusion of minds and often to the crushing of hearts.

Of the other papers I have nothing special to say. They are what they are, and I am by now too hardened a sinner to feel ashamed of insignificant indiscretions. And as to their appearance in this form I claim that indulgence to which all sinners against themselves are entitled.

1920.                                          J. C.

# APPENDICES

*The original prefaces of*
## A PERSONAL RECORD
*and* VICTORY

*A Chronological List of the*
*Published Works of*
*Joseph Conrad*

# SOME REMINISCENCES*

## A FAMILIAR PREFACE

As a general rule we do not want much encouragement to talk about ourselves; yet this little book is the result of a friendly suggestion, and even of a little friendly pressure. I defended myself with some spirit; but, with characteristic tenacity, the friendly voice insisted, 'You know, you really must.'

It was not an argument, but I submitted at once. If one must! . . .

You perceive the force of a word. He who wants to persuade should put his trust not in the right argument, but in the right word. The power of sound has always been greater than the power of sense. I don't say this by way of disparagement. It is better for mankind to be impressionable than reflective. Nothing humanly great—great, I mean, as affecting a whole mass of lives —has come from reflection. On the other hand, you cannot fail to see the power of mere words; such words as Glory, for instance, or Pity. I won't mention any more. They are not far to seek. Shouted with perseverance, with ardour, with conviction, these two by their sound alone have set whole nations in motion and upheaved the dry, hard ground on which rests our whole social fabric. There's 'virtue' for you if you like! . . . Of course the accent must be attended to. The right accent. That's very important. The capacious lung, the thundering or the tender vocal chords. Don't talk to me of your Archimedes' lever. He was an absent-minded person

*A Personal Record was first published in 1912 under this title

O

with a mathematical imagination.  Mathematics command all my respect, but I have no use for engines.  Give me the right word and the right accent and I will move the world.

What a dream for a writer!  Because written words have their accent, too.  Yes!  Let me only find the right word!  Surely it must be lying somewhere among the wreckage of all the plaints and all the exultations poured out aloud since the first day when hope, the undying, came down on earth.  It may be there, close by, disregarded, invisible, quite at hand.  But it's no good. I believe there are men who can lay hold of a needle in a pottle of hay at the first try.  For myself, I have never had such luck.

And then there is that accent.  Another difficulty. For who is going to tell whether the accent is right or wrong till the word is shouted, and fails to be heard, perhaps, and goes down-wind, leaving the world unmoved? Once upon a time there lived an emperor who was a sage and something of a literary man.  He jotted down on ivory tablets thoughts, maxims, reflections which chance has preserved for the edification of posterity. Among other sayings—I am quoting from memory—I remember this solemn admonition: 'Let all thy words have the accent of heroic truth.'  The accent of heroic truth!  This is very fine, but I am thinking that it is an easy matter for an austere emperor to jot down grandiose advice.  Most of the working truths on this earth are humble, not heroic; and there have been times in the history of mankind when the accents of heroic truth have moved it to nothing but derision.

Nobody will expect to find between the covers of this

little book words of extraordinary potency or accents of irresistible heroism. However humiliating for my self-esteem, I must confess that the counsels of Marcus Aurelius are not for me. They are more fit for a moralist than for an artist. Truth of a modest sort I can promise you, and also sincerity. That complete, praiseworthy sincerity which, while it delivers one into the hands of one's enemies, is as likely as not to embroil one with one's friends.

'Embroil' is perhaps too strong an expression. I can't imagine among either my enemies or my friends a being so hard up for something to do as to quarrel with me. 'To disappoint one's friends' would be nearer the mark. Most, almost all, friendships of the writing period of my life have come to me through my books; and I know that a novelist lives in his work. He stands there, the only reality in an invented world, among imaginary things, happenings, and people. Writing about them, he is only writing about himself. But the disclosure is not complete. He remains, to a certain extent, a figure behind the veil; a suspected rather than a seen presence—a movement and a voice behind the draperies of fiction. In these personal notes there is no such veil. And I cannot help thinking of a passage in the *Imitation of Christ* where the ascetic author, who knew life so profoundly, says that 'there are persons esteemed on their reputation who by showing themselves destroy the opinion one had of them.' This is the danger incurred by an author of fiction who sets out to talk about himself without disguise.

While these reminiscent pages were appearing serially I was remonstrated with for bad economy; as if such writing were a form of self-indulgence wasting the

o*

substance of future volumes.   It seems that I am not sufficiently literary.   Indeed, a man who never wrote a line
for print till he was thirty-six cannot bring himself to look
upon his existence and his experience, upon the sum of
his thoughts, sensations, and emotions, upon his memories
and his regrets, and the whole possession of his past, as
only so much material for his hands.   Once before, some
three years ago, when I published *The Mirror of the Sea*, a
volume of impressions and memories, the same remarks
were made to me.   Practical remarks.   But, truth to say,
I have never understood the kind of thrift they recom-
mend.   I wanted to pay my tribute to the sea, its ships
and its men, to whom I remain indebted for so much
which has gone to make me what I am.   That seemed
to me the only shape in which I could offer it to their
shades.   There could not be a question in my mind of anything else.   It is quite possible that I am a bad economist;
but it is certain that I am incorrigible.

Having matured in the surroundings and under the
special conditions of sea life, I have a special piety toward
that form of my past; for its impressions were vivid, its
appeal direct, its demands such as could be responded to with
the natural elation of youth and strength equal to the call.
There was nothing in them to perplex a young conscience.
Having broken away from my origins under a storm of
blame from every quarter which had the merest shadow of
right to voice an opinion, removed by great distances
from such natural affections as were still left to me, and
even estranged, in a measure, from them by the totally
unintelligible character of the life which had seduced me
so mysteriously from my allegiance, I may safely say that
through the blind force of circumstances the sea was to

be all my world and the merchant service my only home for a long succession of years. No wonder, then, that in my two exclusively sea books—*The Nigger of the 'Narcissus'* and *The Mirror of the Sea* (and in the few short sea stories like *Youth* and *Typhoon*)—I have tried with an almost filial regard to render the vibration of life in the great world of waters, in the hearts of the simple men who have for ages traversed its solitudes, and also that something sentient which seems to dwell in ships—the creatures of their hands and the objects of their care.

One's literary life must turn frequently for sustenance to memories and seek discourse with the shades, unless one has made up one's mind to write only in order to reprove mankind for what it is, or praise it for what it is not, or—generally—to teach it how to behave. Being neither quarrelsome, nor a flatterer, nor a sage, I have done none of these things, and I am prepared to put up serenely with the insignificance which attaches to persons who are not meddlesome in some way or other. But resignation is not indifference. I would not like to be left standing as a mere spectator on the bank of the great stream carrying onward so many lives. I would fain claim for myself the faculty of so much insight as can be expressed in a voice of sympathy and compassion.

It seems to me that in one, at least, authoritative quarter of criticism I am suspected of a certain unemotional, grim acceptance of facts — of what the French would call *sécheresse du cœur*. Fifteen years of unbroken silence before praise or blame testify sufficiently to my respect for criticism, that fine flower of personal expression in the garden of letters. But this is more of a personal matter, reaching the man behind the work, and therefore it may be alluded to in a volume which is a personal note in the margin of the public page. Not that I feel hurt in the least. The charge—if it amounted to a charge at all——was made in the most considerate terms; in a tone of regret.

My answer is that if it be true that every novel contains an element of autobiography—and this can hardly be denied, since the creator can only express himself in his creation—then there are some of us to whom an open display of sentiment is repugnant. I would not unduly praise the virtue of restraint. It is often merely temperamental. But it is not always a sign of coldness. It may be pride. There can be nothing more humiliating than to see the shaft of one's emotion miss the mark of either laughter or tears. Nothing more humiliating! And this for the reason that should the mark be missed, should the open display of emotion fail to move, then it must perish unavoidably in disgust or contempt. No artist can be reproached for shrinking from a risk which only fools run to meet and only genius dare confront with impunity. In a task which mainly consists in laying one's soul more or less bare to the world, a regard for decency, even at the cost of success, is but the regard for one's own dignity which is inseparably united with the dignity of one's work.

And then—it is very difficult to be wholly joyous or wholly sad on this earth. The comic, when it is human, soon takes upon itself a face of pain; and some of our griefs (some only, not all, for it is the capacity for suffering which makes man august in the eyes of men) have their source in weaknesses which must be recognized with smiling compassion as the common inheritance of us all.

Joy and sorrow in this world pass into each other, mingling
their forms and their murmurs in the twilight of life as
mysterious as an overshadowed ocean, while the dazzling
brightness of supreme hopes lies far off, fascinating and
still, on the distant edge of the horizon.

Yes!  I, too, would like to hold the magic wand giving
that command over laughter and tears which is declared
to be the highest achievement of imaginative literature.
Only, to be a great magician one must surrender oneself
to occult and irresponsible powers, either outside or
within one's breast.  We have all heard of simple men
selling their souls for love or power to some grotesque
devil.  The most ordinary intelligence can perceive without much reflection that anything of the sort is bound to
be a fool's bargain.  I don't lay claim to particular wisdom
because of my dislike and distrust of such transactions.
It may be my sea training acting upon a natural disposition
to keep good hold on the one thing really mine, but the
fact is that I have a positive horror of losing even for one
moving moment that full possession of myself which is the
first condition of good service.  And I have carried my
notion of good service from my earlier into my later
existence.  I, who have never sought in the written word
anything else but a form of the Beautiful—I have carried
over that article of creed from the decks of ships to the
more circumscribed space of my desk, and by that act,
I suppose, I have become permanently imperfect in the
eyes of the ineffable company of pure aesthetes.

As in political so in literary action a man wins friends
for himself mostly by the passion of his prejudices and
by the consistent narrowness of his outlook.  But I have
never been able to love what was not lovable or hate

what was not hateful out of deference for some general principle. Whether there be any courage in making this admission I know not. After the middle turn of life's way we consider dangers and joys with a tranquil mind. So I proceed in peace to declare that I have always suspected in the effort to bring into play the extremities of emotions the debasing touch of insincerity. In order to move others deeply we must deliberately allow ourselves to be carried away beyond the bounds of our normal sensibility—innocently enough, perhaps, and of necessity, like an actor who raises his voice on the stage above the pitch of natural conversation—but still we have to do that. And surely this is no great sin. But the danger lies in the writer becoming the victim of his own exaggeration, losing the exact notion of sincerity, and in the end coming to despise truth itself as something too cold, too blunt for his purpose—as, in fact, not good enough for his insistent emotion. From laughter and tears the descent is easy to snivelling and giggles.

These may seem selfish considerations; but you can't, in sound morals, condemn a man for taking care of his own integrity. It is his clear duty. And least of all can you condemn an artist pursuing, however humbly and imperfectly, a creative aim. In that interior world where his thought and his emotions go seeking for the experience of imagined adventures, there are no policemen, no law, no pressure of circumstance or dread of opinion to keep him within bounds. Who then is going to say Nay to his temptations if not his conscience?

And besides—this, remember, is the place and the moment of perfectly open talk—I think that all ambitions are lawful except those which climb upward on the miseries or credulities of mankind. All intellectual and artistic ambitions are permissible, up to and even beyond the limit of prudent sanity. They can hurt no one. If they are mad, then so much the worse for the artist. Indeed, as virtue is said to be, such ambitions are their own reward. Is it such a very mad presumption to believe in the sovereign power of one's art, to try for other means, for other ways of affirming this belief in the deeper appeal of one's work? To try to go deeper is not to be insensible. An historian of hearts is not an historian of emotions, yet he penetrates further, restrained as he may be, since his aim is to reach the very fount of laughter and tears. The sight of human affairs deserves admiration and pity. They are worthy of respect, too. And he is not insensible who pays them the undemonstrative tribute of a sigh which is not a sob, and of a smile which is not a grin. Resignation, not mystic, not detached, but resignation open-eyed, conscious, and informed by love, is the only one of our feelings for which it is impossible to become a sham.

Not that I think resignation the last word of wisdom. I am too much the creature of my time for that. But I think that the proper wisdom is to will what the gods will without, perhaps, being certain what their will is— or even if they have a will of their own. And in this matter of life and art it is not the Why that matters so much to our happiness as the How. As the Frenchman said : 'Il y a toujours la manière.' Very true. Yes. There is the manner. The manner in laughter, in tears, in irony, in indignations and enthusiasms, in judgments —and even in love. The manner in which, as in the features and character of a human face, the inner truth is foreshadowed for those who know how to look at their kind.

Those who read me know my conviction that the world, the temporal world, rests on a few very simple ideas; so simple that they must be as old as the hills. It rests notably, among others, on the idea of Fidelity. At a time when nothing which is not revolutionary in some way or other can expect to attract much attention I have not been revolutionary in my writings. The revolutionary spirit is mighty convenient in this, that it frees one from all scruples as regards ideas. Its hard, absolute optimism is repulsive to my mind by the menace of fanaticism and intolerance it contains. No doubt one should smile at these things; but, imperfect Aesthete, I am no better Philosopher. All claim to special righteousness awakens in me that scorn and anger from which a philosophical mind should be free. . . .

I fear that trying to be conversational I have only managed to be unduly discursive. I have never been very well acquainted with the art of conversation—that art which, I understand, is supposed to be lost now. My young days, the days when one's habits and character are formed, have been rather familiar with long silences. Such voices as broke into them were anything but conversational. No. I haven't got the habit. Yet this discursiveness is not so irrelevant to the handful of pages which follow. They, too, have been charged with discursiveness, with disregard of chronological order (which is in itself a crime), with unconventionality of form (which is an impropriety). I was told severely that the public would view with displeasure the informal character of my recollections. 'Alas!' I protested, mildly. 'Could I begin with the sacramental words, "I was born on such a date in such a place"? The remoteness of the locality would have robbed the statement of all interest. I haven't lived through wonderful adventures to be related *seriatim*. I haven't known distinguished men on whom I could pass fatuous remarks. I haven't been mixed up with great or scandalous affairs. This is but a bit of psychological document, and even so, I haven't written it with a view to put forward any conclusion of my own.'

But my objector was not placated. These were good reasons for not writing at all—not a defence of what stood written already, he said.

I admit that almost anything, anything in the world, would serve as a good reason for not writing at all. But since I have written them, all I want to say in their defence is that these memories put down without any regard for established conventions have not been thrown off without system and purpose. They have their hope and their aim. The hope that from the reading of these pages there may emerge at last the vision of a personality; the man behind the books so fundamentally dissimilar as, for instance, *Almayer's Folly* and *The Secret Agent*, and yet a coherent, justifiable personality both in its origin and in its action. This is the hope. The immediate aim, closely associated with the hope, is to give the record of personal memories by presenting faithfully the feelings and sensations connected with the writing of my first book and with my first contact with the sea.

In the purposely mingled resonance of this double strain a friend here and there will perhaps detect a subtle accord.

J. C.

# VICTORY

The last word of this novel was written on the 29th of
May 1914. And that last word was the single word of
the title.

Those were the times of peace. Now that the moment
of publication approaches I have been considering the
discretion of altering the title-page. The word *Victory*,
the shining and tragic goal of noble effort, appeared too
great, too august, to stand at the head of a mere novel.
There was also the possibility of falling under the suspicion
of commercial astuteness deceiving the public into the
belief that the book had something to do with war.

Of that, however, I was not afraid very much. What
influenced my decision most were the obscure promptings
of that pagan residuum of awe and wonder which lurks
still at the bottom of our old humanity. *Victory* was
the last word I had written in peace time. It was the last
literary thought which had occurred to me before the
doors of the Temple of Janus flying open with a crash
shook the minds, the hearts, the consciences of men all
over the world. Such coincidence could not be treated
lightly. And I made up my mind to let the word stand,
in the same hopeful spirit in which some simple citizen
of Old Rome would have 'accepted the omen.'

The second point on which I wish to offer a remark
is the existence (in the novel) of a person named Schomberg.

That I believe him to be true goes without saying.

I am not likely to offer pinchbeck wares to my public consciously. Schomberg is an old member of my company. A very subordinate personage in *Lord Jim* as far back as the year 1899, he became notably active in a certain short story of mine published in 1902. Here he appears in a still larger part, true to life (I hope), but also true to himself. Only, in this instance, his deeper passions come into play, and thus his grotesque psychology is completed at last.

I don't pretend to say that this is the entire Teutonic psychology; but it is indubitably the psychology of a Teuton. My object in mentioning him here is to bring out the fact that, far from being the incarnation of recent animosities, he is the creature of my old, deep-seated and, as it were, impartial conviction.

                                                                J. C.

# A CHRONOLOGICAL LIST OF THE PUBLISHED WORKS OF JOSEPH CONRAD

Joseph Conrad [Teodor Jósef Konrad Nałęcz Korzeni-owski] was born at Bordiczew in the Ukraine on 3rd December 1857. His father, Apollo Nałęcz Korzeniowski, was a gifted poet and translator, whose productions included Polish versions of Shakespeare's *Othello* and *As You Like It*. His mother, Ewelina Bobrowska, having died in exile in 1865, Conrad was sent, in 1867, to the Polish High School at Lemberg. Delicacy of health interfered with his schooling, and in 1870 he was placed in the charge of a private tutor. Accompanied by his tutor, he made a tour in Germany, Switzerland, and Italy.

Bent on a seafaring life, he served his apprenticeship in the French Marine from 1874 to 1877. He first landed in England in 1878; and, after seven years spent chiefly in Indian and Australian waters, became a naturalized British subject in 1885. Having finally abandoned his seafaring life in 1895, he was married in the following year to Miss Jessie George. They had two sons: Boris, born in 1898, and John Alexander, born in 1906.

Conrad's literary career began with a short story, 'The Black Mate,' published in *Tit-Bits* in 1886. His first novel, *Almayer's Folly*, appeared in 1895. The rest of his life was exclusively devoted to literature: he produced some sixty volumes, of which a chronological list is given. He died near Canterbury, Kent, on 3rd August 1924.

(1) *Almayer's Folly: A Story of an Eastern River* (T. Fisher Unwin: London, 1895). (2) *An Outcast of the Islands* (T. Fisher Unwin: London, 1896). (3) *The Children of the Sea: A Tale of the Forecastle* (Dodd, Mead & Co.: New York, 1897); the first English edition was published under the title of *The Nigger of the 'Narcissus': A Tale of the Sea* (William Heinemann: London, 1898). (4) *Tales of Unrest* [*Karain, The Idiots, An Outpost of Progress, The Return, The Lagoon*] (T. Fisher Unwin: London, 1898). (5) *Lord Jim: A Tale* (William Blackwood & Sons: Edinburgh and London, 1900). (6) *The Inheritors: An Extravagant Story* [written in collaboration with Ford Madox Hueffer] (McClure, Phillips & Co.: New York, 1901; William Heinemann: London, 1901). (7) *Youth: A Narrative, and Two other Stories* [*Heart of Darkness, The End of the Tether*] (William Blackwood & Sons: Edinburgh and London, 1902). (8) *Typhoon* (G. P. Putnam's Sons: New York and London, 1902); the first English edition was published under the title of *Typhoon, and other Stories* [*Amy Foster, To-morrow, Falk*] (William Heinemann: London, 1903). (9) *Romance: A Novel* [written in collaboration with Ford Madox Hueffer] (Smith, Elder & Co.: London, 1903; McClure, Phillips & Co.: New York, 1904). (10) *Nostromo: A Tale of the Seaboard* (Harper & Brothers: London and New York, 1904). (11) *The Mirror of the Sea: Memories and Impressions* (Methuen & Co.: London, 1906; Harper & Brothers: New York, 1906). (12) *The Secret Agent: A Simple Tale* (Methuen & Co.: London, 1907; Harper & Brothers: New York, 1907). (13) *A Set of Six* [*Gaspar Ruiz, The Informer, The Brute, An Anarchist, The Duel, Il Conde*] (Methuen & Co.: London, 1908; Doubleday, Page & Co.: New York, 1915). (14) *Under Western Eyes* (Methuen & Co.: London, 1911; Harper & Brothers: New York, 1911). (15) *Some Reminiscences* (Eveleigh Nash: London, 1912); the first United States edition was published under the title of *A Personal Record* (Harper & Brothers: New York, 1912). (16) *'Twixt Land and Sea: Tales* [*A Smile of Fortune, The Secret*

*Sharer, Freya of the Seven Islands*] (J. M. Dent & Sons: London, 1912; The George H. Doran Co.: New York, 1912). (17) *Chance: A Tale in Two Parts* (Methuen & Co.: London, 1913; Doubleday, Page & Co.: New York, 1914). (18) *Within the Tides: Tales* [*The Planter of Malata, The Partner, The Inn of the Two Witches, Because of the Dollars*] (J. M. Dent & Sons: London and Toronto, 1915). (19) *Victory: An Island Tale* (Doubleday, Page & Co.: New York, 1915; Methuen & Co.: London, 1915). (20) *One Day More: A Play in One Act* (Privately printed by Clement Shorter: London, 1917); an edition was issued by the Beaumont Press in 1919. (21) *The Shadow-Line: A Confession* (J. M. Dent & Sons: London and Toronto, 1917; Doubleday, Page & Co.: New York, 1917). (22) *'Well done!'* (Privately printed by Clement Shorter: London, 1918); included in *Notes on Life and Letters* (1921). (23) *The First News* (Privately printed by Clement Shorter: London, 1918); included in *Notes on Life and Letters* (1921). (24) *The Tale* (Privately printed by Clement Shorter: London, 1919). (25) *London's River* (Privately printed by Clement Shorter: London, 1919). (26) *The Shock of War: Through Germany to Cracow* (Printed for private circulation: London, 1919); included in *Notes on Life and Letters* (1921). (27) *To Poland in War-time: A Journey into the East* (Printed for private circulation: London, 1919); included in *Notes on Life and Letters* (1921). (28) *The North Sea on the Eve of War* (Printed for private circulation: London, 1919); included in *Notes on Life and Letters* (1921). (29) *My Return to Cracow* (Printed for private circulation: London, 1919); included in *Notes on Life and Letters* (1921). (30) *Tradition* (Printed for private circulation only: London, 1919); included in *Notes on Life and Letters* (1921). (31) *The Polish Question: A Note on the joint Protectorate of the Western Powers and Russia* (Privately printed by Clement Shorter: London, 1919). (32) *Some Reflexions, Seamanlike and otherwise, on the loss of the 'Titanic'* (Printed for private circulation only: London, 1919); included in *Notes on Life and Letters* (1921).

(33) *Some Aspects of the Admirable Inquiry into the Loss of the 'Titanic'* (Printed for private circulation only: London, 1919); included in *Notes on Life and Letters* (1921).    (34) *The Arrow of Gold: A Story between Two Notes* (Doubleday, Page & Co.: New York, 1919; T. Fisher Unwin: London, 1919).    (35) *Autocracy and War* (Printed for private circulation: London, 1919).    (36) *Guy de Maupassant* (Printed for private circulation: London, 1919); included in *Notes on Life and Letters* (1921).    (37) *Henry James: An Appreciation* (Printed for private circulation: London, 1919); included in *Notes on Life and Letters* (1921).    (38) *Anatole France* [A review of Anatole France's novel *Crainquebille*] (Printed for Joseph Conrad, Orlestone, by Richard Clay & Sons: London, 1919); included in *Notes on Life and Letters* (1921).    (39) *Tales of the Sea* [A criticism of Marryat and Fenimore Cooper] (Printed for Joseph Conrad, Orlestone, by Richard Clay & Sons: London, 1919); included in *Notes on Life and Letters* (1921).    (40) *The Lesson of the Collision: A Monograph upon the Loss of the 'Empress of Ireland'* (Printed for Joseph Conrad, Orlestone, by Richard Clay & Sons: London, 1919); included in *Notes on Life and Letters* (1921).    (41) *An Observer in Malay* (Printed for the Author for private circulation only by Richard Clay & Sons: London, 1920); included in *Notes on Life and Letters* (1921).    (42) *Books* (Printed for the Author by Richard Clay & Sons: London, 1920); included in *Notes on Life and Letters* (1921).    (43) *Alphonse Daudet* (Printed for the Author by Richard Clay & Sons: London, 1920); included in *Notes on Life and Letters* (1921).    (44) *Prince Roman* (Printed for the Author by Richard Clay & Sons: London, 1920).    (45) *The Warrior's Soul* (Printed for the Author for private circulation by Richard Clay & Sons: London, 1920).    (46) *Confidence* (Printed for the Author by Richard Clay & Sons: London, 1920); included in *Notes on Life and Letters* (1921).    (47) *Anatole France: L'Île des Pingouins* (Printed for the Author by Richard Clay & Sons: London, 1920); included in *Notes on Life and Letters* (1921).    (48) *The Rescue: A Romance of the Shallows* (Doubleday, Page & Co.:

New York, 1920; J. M. Dent & Sons: London and Toronto, 1920). (49) *Notes on Life and Letters* (J. M. Dent & Sons: London and Toronto, 1921). (50) *Notes on my Books* (William Heinemann: London, 1921; Doubleday, Page & Co.: New York and Toronto, 1921). (51) *The Secret Agent: A Drama in Four Acts* (Printed for the Author by H. J. Goulden Ltd.: Canterbury, 1921). (52) *The Black Mate: A Story* (Printed for the Author for private distribution only: 1922). (53) *John Galsworthy: An Appreciation* (Printed for private circulation by H. J. Goulden Ltd.: Canterbury, 1922). (54) *The Dover Patrol: A Tribute* (Printed for private circulation by H. J. Goulden Ltd.: Canterbury, 1922). (55) *The Rover* (T. Fisher Unwin: London, 1923; Doubleday, Page & Co.: New York, 1923). (56) *Laughing Anne: A Play* (London, 1923). (57) *The 'Torrens': A Personal Tribute* (Privately printed by F. A. Hook: 1923). (58) *The Nature of a Crime* [written in collaboration with Ford Madox Hueffer] (Duckworth & Co.: London, 1924). (59) *Geography and Some Explorers* (Privately printed by Strangeways & Sons: London, 1924). (60) *Five Letters . . . written to Edward Noble in 1895. With a Foreword by Edward Noble* (Privately printed: London, 1925). (61) *Admiralty Paper* (Privately printed for Jerome Kern: 1925). (62) *Suspense: A Napoleonic Novel* (Doubleday, Page & Co.: New York, 1925; J. M. Dent & Sons: London and Toronto, 1925). (63) *Tales of Hearsay . . . With a Preface by R. B. Cunninghame Graham* (T. Fisher Unwin: London, 1925). (64) *Last Essays* (J. M. Dent & Sons: London and Toronto, 1926). (65) *Joseph Conrad's Diary of his Journey up the Valley of the Congo in 1890. With an Introduction and Notes by Richard Curle* (Privately printed: London, 1926). (66) *Joseph Conrad's Letters to his Wife* (Privately printed: London, 1927). (67) [Letters, about 600 in number, published in] *Joseph Conrad: Life and Letters* (Doubleday, Page & Co.: New York, 1927; William Heinemann: London, 1927. 2 vols.), by G. Jean-Aubry. (68) *Letters from Conrad, 1895–1924. Edited with Introduction and Notes by Edward Garnett* (The Nonesuch

Press: London, 1928; The Bobbs-Merrill Co.: Indianapolis, 1928). (69) *Letters from Joseph Conrad to Richard Curle*. *Edited with an Introduction and Notes by R. C.* (Sampson Low, Marston & Co.: London, 1928; Doubleday-Doran: New York, 1928).